Praise for Mike Zdeb

Anyone who has ever tried to create a map using SAS and ended up with a skewed, backwards view of the world will appreciate Mike Zdeb's book, *Maps Made Easy Using SAS®*. This book is a clear, succinct primer and reference tool on creating maps within SAS. Experienced SAS users will find the book a breeze to use and will quickly gain from its in-depth examples. Novices can type in the examples and follow the numbered points explaining the lines of code and easily follow the map-creation logic. The multiple examples build upon each other, producing more complex maps, and pull together and explain the sundry SAS commands involved.

The first few chapters take the reader quickly into the world of map-making in SAS. Later chapters go into detail on how to create complicated choropleth maps, although most examples and instructions can be easily adapted for other types of SAS maps. Even Web-ready maps using JAVA and ACTIVEX are covered, showing drill-down and pop-up capabilities.

Russell Adair, Ph.D.
Associate Director
Office of Institutional Research
Yale University

Ssas. | SAS Publishing

Maps Made Easy Using SAS®

ART CARPENTER'S SAS® SOFTWARE SERIES

Mike Zdeb

The Power to Know™

Table of Contents

Appendix

Preface

Information can have many associations—entities (people, places, things), time, and space. The spatial component of information is often illustrated with a map. Sometimes the creation of a map requires a geographic information system (GIS). This book demonstrates that there are many instances where SAS/GRAPH software can produce maps that are perfectly acceptable alternatives to what is possible with GIS software. In fact, some features of SAS/GRAPH, such as map animation, go beyond normal GIS capabilities.

This book is intended for a variety of users. If you have not used SAS/GRAPH software, or if you have used SAS/GRAPH but not the GMAP procedure, there is introductory material that will show you how to produce maps. If you already know how to produce maps but have wondered how to enhance them with features such as labels for map areas or an inset that zooms in on a section of the map, you'll learn how to add these enhancements. If you already are an experienced map maker with SAS/GRAPH, you can learn how to share your information with others on the World Wide Web with maps that feature drill-down map areas and/or legends; pop-ups that can provide additional information about map areas or map features; and animation that allows a user of your information to cycle through a series of maps.

Acknowledgments

I have organized these acknowledgments longitudinally—not in space, but in time. My many questions about the computing environment at my workplace, the Center for Community Health, have always been patiently answered by the computer science staff at the New York State Department of Health. Questions from both staff at the health department and my students at the School of Public Health helped me understand what I do and do not know about SAS and SAS/GRAPH. SAS Technical Support (especially Martin Mincey) has provided either solutions or workarounds when I have hit dead ends in trying to work out problems on my own. My reviewers (especially Warren Repole and Marcia Surratt) offered many helpful suggestions concerning both my writing and technical details pertaining to my SAS code. My first editor, Judy Whatley, provided the necessary encouragement for me to keep going after I had almost given up this project. My current editor, Stephenie Joyner, has shown patience without bounds, and has also been instrumental in my completing this book. Finally, thanks to my first (and current) wife, Kathy (more of a writer than I can ever hope to be), whose well-spaced combination of both needling and encouraging words got me to devote the time I needed to finish my writing and editing.

x

Using This Book

The chapters are organized to introduce new concepts in a progressively more advanced manner, and all concepts are illustrated with examples. The majority of the examples use population data from the United States 2000 census.

Chapters 1 and 2 are intended for the beginning map maker (or those new to SAS/GRAPH). Chapter 1 introduces the GMAP procedure and shows examples of the four basic map types (choropleth, prism, block, surface), using the same data for each map type. Several other procedures (GREMOVE, GRPROJECT, GREDUCE) that complement PROC GMAP are described. Chapter 2 concentrates on choropleth maps, though many of the concepts that are discussed are applicable to other map types. The examples focus on changing the appearance of maps by modifying features such as text and patterns used to fill map areas.

Chapters 3 and 4 introduce advanced topics. In Chapter 3, maps are enhanced using either GMAP procedure options or options in combination with DATA steps or other graphics procedures. Chapter 4 illustrates how to use the Annotate facility to customize maps by adding various features such as labels for map areas and symbols to show the location of cities.

Chapter 5 explains how to share your maps with others, either in hardcopy form or by posting them on the Web. A number of recently introduced SAS/GRAPH features for Web-posted graphics are illustrated.

Finally, an appendix contains information about the data used in all the examples, plus some SAS jobs that assist you in using the material presented in the five chapters. *Note: When you run the book's examples, you can create the text and legends shown in many of the figures by using the GOPTIONS and LEGEND statements included in Appendix A3.*

To find more mapping examples, download updates to SAS/GRAPH mapping data sets, and keep up with the most current mapping tools, go to **www.sas.com/mapsonline**.

CHAPTER 1

Introduction

1.1 Chapter Overview

You can create maps with SAS by using PROC GMAP, one of the procedures available within SAS/GRAPH. Like other SAS procedures, PROC GMAP can be used on a number of levels. At a beginning level, you can produce a number of different types of maps using very little SAS code and no procedure options. At a more advanced level, you can create maps with labeled areas and hyperlinks to other information. This chapter introduces basic topics: the data needed to create maps, the various types of maps that can be produced, and some other SAS/GRAPH procedures that complement PROC GMAP.

1.2 Data Sets Needed to Produce a Map

You produce maps with PROC GMAP by using a combination of a map data set and a response data set. A map data set contains the information needed to draw map boundaries. Some typical map boundaries are defined by country, state, county, census tract, and zip code. A response data set contains the information that is to be displayed on the map, such as country-specific birth rates or state-specific populations.

The work that PROC GMAP performs is analogous to that performed by a match-merge in a DATA step. A match-merge combines observations from two or more data sets using one or more BY variables to match like observations. PROC GMAP matches observations from a response data set to those in a map data set using one or more ID variables. A DATA step match-merge results in a new data set, while PROC GMAP results in a geographical display of your response data.

1.2.1 Map Data Sets

In addition to giving you the graphics procedures that allow you to work with geographic-based data, SAS/GRAPH also provides map data sets that allow you to create at least one map of nearly every country in the world. The map data sets provided with SAS/GRAPH contain geographic areas (boundaries) represented in terms of longitude and latitude. At a minimum, the map data sets contain three variables: the two coordinates for the points of area boundaries, and a variable that contains a value for the geographic area associated with each set of coordinates. The variables that contain the coordinates used by PROC GMAP to draw maps must be numeric and must be named X (longitude) and Y (latitude). The variable that contains the value of the geographic areas is referred to as the identification variable. Its name varies among the map data sets; in some map data sets, a given set of coordinates may be associated with more than one geographic area (such as a state and a county). The map data sets are stored in the MAPS library, located in the directory MAPS under the SAS root directory. You can use the libref MAPS without having to use a LIBNAME statement. You can use any of the map data sets supplied by SAS in PROC GMAP by specifying a two-level data set name, such as MAPS.US or MAPS.USCOUNTY.

SAS/GRAPH provides several map data sets that you can use to draw maps of the United States. The US data set contains the following variables:

VARIABLE	TYPE	LABEL
SEGMENT	Num	State Segment Number
STATE	Num	State FIPS Code
X	Num	X Coordinate
Y	Num	Y Coordinate

In this data set, the variable STATE is the geographic area associated with the mapping coordinates. SEGMENT is another variable in this data set that is common to many of the map data sets. That variable is used by PROC GMAP to draw geographic areas that may comprise more than one polygon and still identify the multiple polygons as representing only one area. An example of such an occurrence in the US data set is the state of Hawaii, which is made up of several islands.

You can also use the USCOUNTY data set to draw a map of the United States. It is an example of a data set in which each set of coordinates is associated with more than one geographic area. The data set contains the following variables:

VARIABLE	TYPE	LABEL
COUNTY	Num	County FIPS Code
SEGMENT	Num	County Segment Number
STATE	Num	State FIPS Code
X	Num	X Coordinate
Y	Num	Y Coordinate

The addition of the variable COUNTY enables you to draw maps of the United States that show both state and county boundaries. Additional variables appear in some of the other map data sets. They are discussed later in this chapter, as are attributes of the X-Y coordinate pairs that vary among the map data sets.

1.2.2 Response Data Sets

A response data set contains the data that you want to display in the form of a map. Just as each map data set contains a variable that associates each set of coordinates with a geographic area, each observation to be displayed in a map must also contain a variable that can be used to match it to an area in the map data set. This common variable must have the same name and be of the same type as the variable in the map data set. If the US map data set is being used to draw a map, the numeric variable STATE identifies areas. To display data associated with any of the states, a response data set must also contain a numeric variable named STATE that allows PROC GMAP to match the data to be displayed with the correct map areas.

The response data set (US2000ST) used in most of the examples contains four variables:

VARIABLE	TYPE	LABEL
POP1990	Num	Year 1990 Census Population
POP2000	Num	Year 2000 Census Population
REGION	Char	Census Region
STATE	Num	State FIPS Code

The data set can be created using SAS code and data found in Appendix A1. That SAS code creates a temporary SAS data set, placing it in the WORK library. All the examples assume that this data set is in the WORK library. If you want to create a permanent SAS data set by modifying the code in Appendix A1.1 as follows, then you must also modify the examples to explicitly state the location of the data set US2000ST, a libref other than WORK.

```
libname pop 'd:\census';
data pop.us2000st;
<rest of SAS code>
```

The values of the variable STATE in a response data set must correspond to the values of that variable in the US map data set. The FIPNAME function, supplied by SAS, can be used to display the state name associated with any given FIPS code. (FIPS stands for Federal Information Processing Standards.) SAS code in Appendix A2 shows an easy way to list numeric FIPS codes and names.

1.3 Map Types in PROC GMAP

You can create four different map types using PROC GMAP: choropleth, prism, block, and surface. Your choice of map type depends on the information you want to convey. In some situations, more than one type of map may be appropriate. In others, a given map type may actually hinder understanding of your data. Each of these map types is shown in the following series of examples. The data displayed in each map are the year 2000 census state-specific populations of the United States (data was obtained from the U.S. Census Bureau Web site). As stated in section 1.2, the response data set, US2000ST, to be used in the examples is assumed to be in the WORK library and can be created using the SAS code and data shown in Appendix A1.

1.3.1 Choropleth Maps

A choropleth map uses shading, patterns, or colors to distinguish map areas (in this case, states). In Figure 1.1, four different population levels are shown using shading, with darker shading indicating a higher population. The four levels represent quartiles, or the 51 areas (50 states plus the District of Columbia) divided into four groups of approximately 13 states each.

Example 1.1 Create a choropleth map

```
proc format;   ❶
value pop
low      -< 1300000 = '<1.3'      1300000 -< 4000000 = '1.3-3.9'
4000000 -< 6000000 = '4.0-5.9'  6000000 -  high      = '6.0+'
;
run;
pattern1 v=ms c=grayfa;   ❷
pattern2 v=ms c=grayda;
pattern3 v=ms c=grayaa;
pattern4 v=ms c=gray5a;

title 'YEAR 2000 CENSUS POPULATION';

proc gmap   ❸
map=maps.us
data=us2000st;
id state;   ❹
choro pop2000   ❺ / discrete coutline=black;   ❻
label pop2000='MILLIONS';   ❼
format pop2000 pop.;   ❽
run;
quit;
```

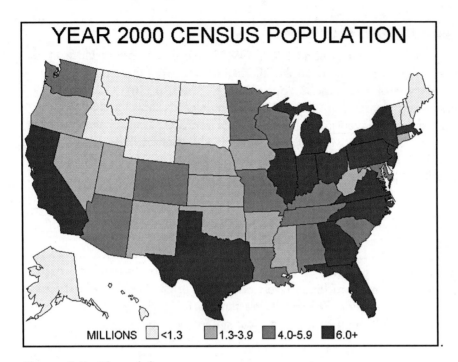

Figure 1.1 *Choropleth map*

This example creates a format, POP,❶ that will be used to group states based on their year 2000 population. Using a format to group geographic areas in a map is no different from grouping observations in the output from other non-graphic procedures. Just as you might use a format to group observations in a table produced using PROC TABULATE, you can use a format to group geographic areas when using PROC GMAP.

You can use a number of methods to represent the four levels of population in the map. One method is to use different hatching patterns—lines drawn within areas at various angles and spacings. Another method is to use color. The method used here is to assign a different gray-scale value to each of four population levels.❷ Patterns have two main attributes: a value, defined here as V=MS, or VALUE=MSOLID; and a color, defined here as C=GRAYxx, or COLOR=GRAYxx. The gray scale in SAS has 256 levels. The xx values following the word GRAY are hexadecimal values that range from 00 (gray00) or black (no color) to FF (grayff) or white (all colors combined; remember what happens when you pass white light through a prism). The four colors shown in the PATTERN statements start at a value close to white (grayfa) and progress to a value closer to black (gray5a).

The US map data set supplied by SAS and the response data set containing the population data are used to create a map.❸ The variable that is common to the two data sets is STATE. If you were match-merging two data sets, you would tell SAS to match observations according to the variable(s) in a BY statement. In PROC GMAP, an ID statement ❹ declares the variable(s) that matches response data set observations to map data set areas.

A CHORO statement ❺ instructs PROC GMAP to create a choropleth map displaying values of the variable POP2000 in the response data set. Two options in the CHORO statement ❻ override the default behavior of PROC GMAP. First, the DISCRETE option treats the response variable (POP2000) as having distinct levels rather than as a continuous variable. The levels are defined in the user-written format POP. Without the DISCRETE option (or the LEVELS option), a formula (shown in PROC GMAP documentation) determines the number of levels used to display values of the response variable. Second, the COUTLINE option results in a map with states outlined in black. Without the COUTLINE option, areas are outlined in the colors specified in the PATTERN statements used to fill map areas. This default behavior may result in map areas that cannot be distinguished from each other if they lie next to each other and have the same color.

PROC GMAP uses the label of the response variable to label the map legend. If no label is present, the name of the variable is used. The LABEL statement ❼ changes the legend label from that in the response data set to "millions." The FORMAT statement ❽ groups the populations in the response data set according to the ranges specified by the format POP.

1.3.2 Prism Maps

In addition to the shading, patterns, and colors used by choropleth maps, a prism map uses the height of raised map areas to convey information. The height of the map areas is proportional to the ordinal level (rank) of the data values in the response data set. Only one change is needed in the SAS code of Example 1.1 to create a prism map instead of a choropleth map. You use the same FORMAT, PATTERN, and TITLE statements. The change is made within PROC GMAP, where the CHORO statement in Example 1.1 has been replaced by a PRISM statement. ❶

Example 1.2 Create a prism map

```
proc format;
value pop
low      -< 1300000 = '<1.3'     1300000 -< 4000000 = '1.3-3.9'
4000000 -< 6000000 = '4.0-5.9'  6000000 -  high     = '6.0+'
;
run;

pattern1 v=ms c=grayfa;
pattern2 v=ms c=grayda;
pattern3 v=ms c=grayaa;
pattern4 v=ms c=gray5a;

title 'YEAR 2000 CENSUS POPULATION';

proc gmap
map=maps.us
data=us2000st
;
```

```
id state;
prism pop2000 ❶   / discrete coutline=black;
label pop2000 = 'MILLIONS';
format pop2000 pop.;
run;
quit;
```

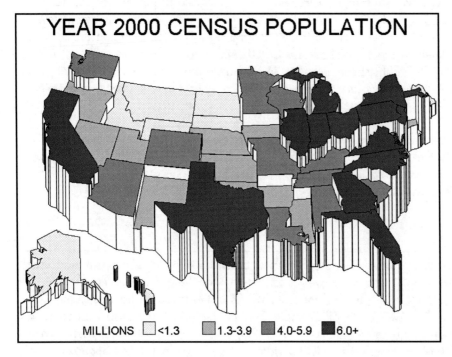

Figure 1.2 *Prism map*

The default map produced by the PRISM statement in this example may obscure some map areas behind other raised areas. You can use several options to alter the viewing angle of a prism map. The default viewing angle is a position above and to the south of the center of the map. You can change three features of the viewing angle using XVIEW (east-west location, default at the map center, 0.5), YVIEW (north-south location, default south of the map, –2.0), and ZVIEW (height above the map, 3.0). The PROC GMAP documentation contains a detailed explanation of the X-Y-Z coordinate system and the X-Y-Z views. Example 1.3 shows the change in the appearance of the prism map if the YVIEW (moved north) and ZVIEW (moved higher) are altered. ❶ Each prism map also has an imagined light source, whose position controls the appearance of the raised edges of the map areas. You can alter the position of the light source using the XLIGHT and YLIGHT options. The map shown in Figure 1.3 contains shading that has been added to the edges of all the map areas by changing the YLIGHT value.❷

Example 1.3 Create a prism map with several options

```
proc format;
value pop
low      -< 1300000 = '<1.3'
1300000 -< 4000000 = '1.3-3.9'
4000000 -< 6000000 = '4.0-5.9'
6000000 -  high     = '6.0+'
;
run;

pattern1 v=ms c=grayfa;
pattern2 v=ms c=grayda;
pattern3 v=ms c=grayaa;
pattern4 v=ms c=gray5a;

title 'YEAR 2000 CENSUS POPULATION';

proc gmap
map=maps.us
data=us2000st
;
id state;
prism pop2000 / discrete coutline=black yview=-0.5 zview=4.0 ❶   ylight=2 ❷;
label pop2000 = 'MILLIONS';
format pop2000 pop.;
run;

quit;
```

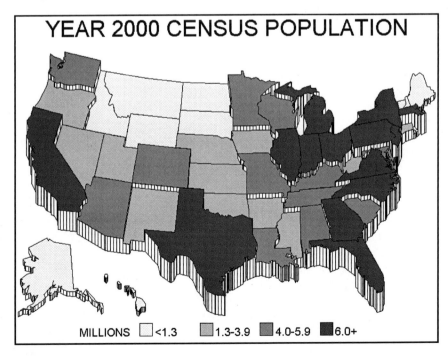

Figure 1.3 *Prism map with modified view and light source*

1.3.3 Block Maps

The block map combines features of choropleth and prism maps. You can distinguish among the map areas because the area boundaries are displayed. However, the map areas are not shaded based on data values. Instead, a block is placed at the center of each map area and the height of that block is the ordinal level (rank) of the response variable. The blocks are also shaded, as with prism maps, where both shading and the height of raised areas convey information about the response variable.

Example 1.4 Create a block map

```
proc format;
value pop
low      -< 1300000 = '<1.3'
1300000 -< 4000000 = '1.3-3.9'
4000000 -< 6000000 = '4.0-5.9'
6000000 -  high     = '6.0+'
;
run;

pattern1 v=s c=grayfa;  ❶
pattern2 v=s c=grayda;
pattern3 v=s c=grayaa;
pattern4 v=s c=gray5a;

title 'YEAR 2000 CENSUS POPULATION';

proc gmap
map=maps.us
data=us2000st
;
id state;
block pop2000 ❷   / discrete coutline=black cblkout=black ❸ ;
label pop2000 = 'MILLIONS';
format pop2000 pop.;
run;
quit;
```

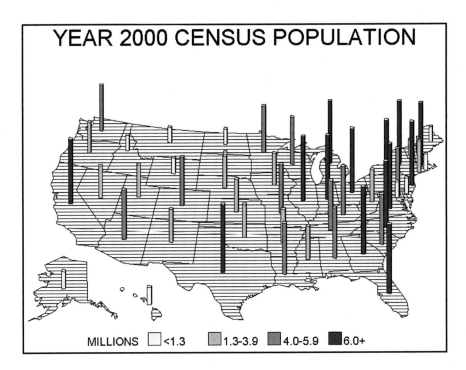

YEAR 2000 CENSUS POPULATION

MILLIONS ☐<1.3 ☐1.3-3.9 ☐4.0-5.9 ■6.0+

Figure 1.4 *Block map*

In this example, the BLOCK statement ❷ creates a map with raised blocks positioned at the center of each map area. The blocks are shaded with grays. The PATTERN statements ❶ are specified as V=S. A value of MS as used in the previous examples controls the fill for map areas, not for the raised blocks. The DISCRETE option plus the FORMAT statement results in blocks drawn at four different heights, proportional to the ordinal level (rank) of the formatted values of the response variable, POPULATION. Blocks are outlined in black ❸ as a result of using the CBLKOUT (color of block outline) option. The fill pattern for the map areas is equally spaced horizontal lines. If no PATTERN statements had been used to specify the fills of the blocks, the map areas would have used the default solid fill.

As with the prism map, you can use options to alter the appearance of the block map. Several of these options are shown in Example 1.5.

Example 1.5 Create a block map with several options

```
proc format;
value pop
low       -< 1300000 = '<1.3'
1300000 -< 4000000 = '1.3-3.9'
4000000 -< 6000000 = '4.0-5.9'
6000000 -  high     = '6.0+'
;
run;

pattern1 v=s c=grayfa;
pattern2 v=s c=grayda;
pattern3 v=s c=grayaa;
pattern4 v=s c=gray5a;
pattern5 v=ms c=grayea;  ❶

title 'YEAR 2000 CENSUS POPULATION';

proc gmap
map=maps.us
data=us2000st
;
id state;
block pop2000 / discrete coutline=black cblkout=black blocksize=6  ❷
shape=prism  ❸
             xview=0.75 yview=-1.0 zview=3.5  ❹  ;
label pop2000 = 'MILLIONS';
format pop2000 pop.;
run;
quit;
```

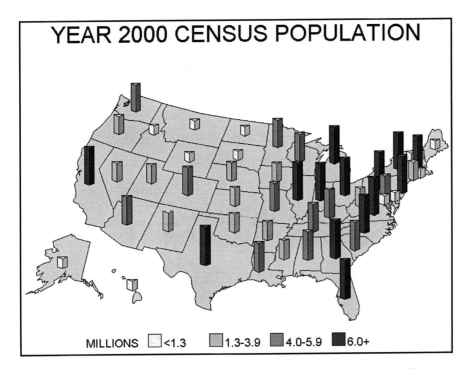

Figure 1.5 *Block map with modified view, block width, and area fill pattern*

This example uses a fifth PATTERN statement to control the fill used for map areas. ❶ Two PATTERN attributes are defined. The value (V) of the PATTERN is MS, not S as was used for the block fill patterns. The prefix M, for map, indicates that this PATTERN is to be used for the map areas. If you wanted an empty pattern, you would use ME to distinguish between a map area pattern and a block fill pattern. The width of the blocks is changed to 6 (from the default value of 2) using the BLOCKSIZE option, ❷ and their SHAPE ❸ is changed from the default block to a prism using the SHAPE= option. The default view is also modified ❹ (as was done with the prism map in Example 1.3). The default view values are the same as with the prism map. Changing the XVIEW to 0.75 from the default 0.50 moves the viewpoint to the east. A YVIEW value of −1.0 moves the viewpoint north from the default −2.0, which lies to the south of the map. Finally, changing the ZVIEW to 3.5 from the default 3.0 moves the viewing position higher over the map.

Rather than displaying discrete values of the response variable, a block map can display blocks used to show relative values of the response variable—that is, taller blocks have higher populations. The map is not intended to allow a viewer to assign a value of the response variable to a given map area.

Example 1.6 Create a continuously scaled response variable

```
pattern1 v=s  c=gray8a r=51; ❶
pattern2 v=ms c=grayea;
title "YEAR 2000 CENSUS POPULATION";

proc gmap
map=maps.us
data=us2000st
;
id state;
block pop2000 / coutline=black nolegend ❷  levels=51 ❸
                blocksize=6 shape=cylinder ❹ ;
run;
quit;
```

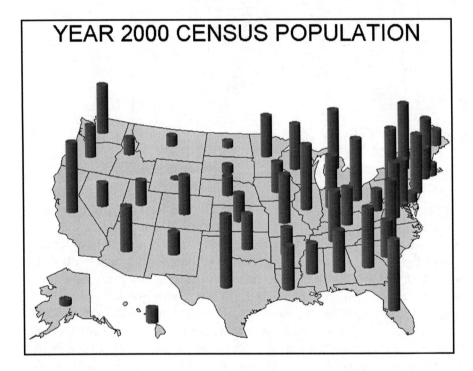

Figure 1.6 *Block map with continuously scaled blocks*

This example uses one pattern for the 51 blocks in the map ❶ by including the R (REPEAT) option in the PATTERN statement. The legend is suppressed ❷ since there is no use for a legend in this type of display. The LEVELS option results in blocks whose heights are scaled continuously from the lowest to the highest value (51 values—one per state plus the District of Columbia) of the response variable. ❸ The SHAPE option specifies the shape of the cylinder chosen for the raised areas. ❹

1.3.4 Surface Maps

The surface map is a departure from the other types of maps in that it does not display the boundaries of map areas. Rather, it uses a spike at the center of each map area, and the heights of the spikes distinguish among values of the data being displayed. The heights of the spikes show relative, not exact, values of the response variable. The choropleth, prism, and block map examples use the DISCRETE option and a format to create four groups of the response variable, POPULATION, and a map with four different gray-scale shadings of either map areas or blocks. A surface map scales the height of map spikes continuously from the lowest to the highest value of the response variable (similar to the block map in Example 1.6). No format is needed to group observations, and no PATTERN statements are needed since the map areas are not shaded.

Example 1.7 Create a surface map

```
title 'YEAR 2000 CENSUS POPULATION';

proc gmap
map=maps.us
data=us2000st
;
id state;
surface pop2000; ❶
run;
quit;
```

The SURFACE statement ❶ creates the map in Figure 1.7. No interior map areas are displayed.

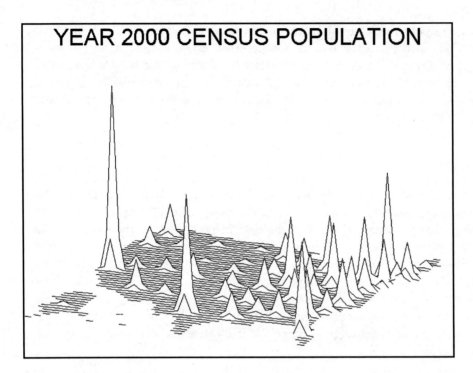

Figure 1.7 *Surface map*

The spikes rise from the center of the map areas to indicate the relative populations of the states. The block map in Figure 1.6 presents a similar display of the population data, created using a LEVELS option. No LEVELS option is available (or needed) when creating a surface map. The intent of a surface map is to show relative values of the response data, and no discrete display is possible.

Several options can alter the appearance of a surface map. The viewing angle is controlled by two options, ROTATE and TILT. The ROTATE option controls the position of the map with respect to the z axis, while the TILT option controls the position of the map with respect to the x axis. The default value of both options is 70 degrees. Higher values of ROTATE turn the map in a counterclockwise direction. TILT can vary from 0 to 90 degrees, or from directly overhead to an edge view, respectively.

Example 1.8 Create a surface map with altered viewing angle

```
title 'YEAR 2000 CENSUS POPULATION';

proc gmap
map=maps.us
data=us2000st
;
id state;
surface pop2000 / rotate=110 tilt=60 ❶ ;
;
run;

quit;
```

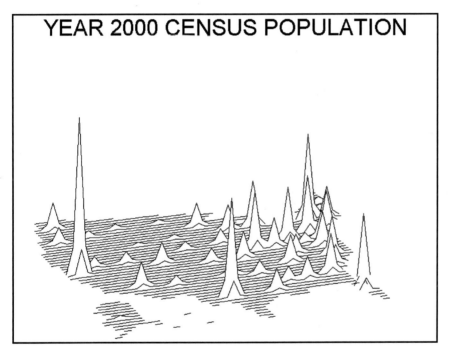

Figure 1.8 *Surface map with altered viewing angle*

In this example, rotating the map 110 degrees (40 degrees beyond the default value) has moved the view in the counterclockwise direction. ❶ The viewing point above the map has risen slightly, from the default of 70 degrees to 60 degrees (remember that 0 degrees is directly above the map).

You can use two other options to change the appearance of the map surface. The NLINES option controls the number of lines used to draw the map surface. The default value is 50, with an allowable range of 50 to 100. The CONSTANT option controls the appearance of the spikes. The default value is 10. Numbers greater than 10 result in spikes that are taller and have a wider base, and numbers less than 10 have the opposite effect.

Example 1.9 Create a surface map with altered viewing angle and map surface

```
title 'YEAR 2000 CENSUS POPULATION';

proc gmap
map=maps.us
data=us2000st
;
id state;
surface pop2000 / rotate=110 tilt=50 ❶  nlines=100 constant=20 ❷  ;
run;
quit;
```

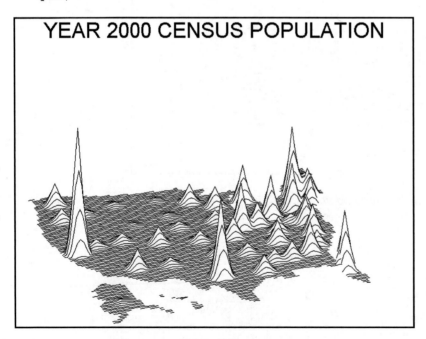

Figure 1.9 *Surface map with altered viewing angle and map surface*

This figure uses the same rotation as in Figure 1.8, but the tilt has been moved higher over the map. ❶ The surface of the map looks more dense. This was accomplished by using the maximum value of the NLINES option. ❷ The appearance of the spikes was also altered by doubling the value of the CONSTANT option from 10 to 20.

1.4 Other Procedures That Use Map Data Sets

Several other SAS/GRAPH procedures use map data sets. Their function is not to draw maps but to work with and modify the existing map data sets, creating new map data sets in the process. The procedures are discussed briefly in this chapter and more extensively in Chapter 3.

1.4.1 PROC GREMOVE

You can use PROC GREMOVE to remove the internal boundaries of a map area, combining already defined map areas (in this example, states) into a larger map area or areas. The US map data set used in all the examples thus far contains internal state boundaries within the mainland portion of the United States. If the state boundaries were removed, you could use PROC GMAP to draw an outline map of the United States.

In addition to a variable (STATE) that associates each X-Y coordinate in the data set with current map areas, the data set must also contain another variable that associates the coordinates with the new map area or areas. Since the US map data set does not contain a variable with a single value common to all observations in the data set, you can use a DATA step to add that variable to the data set.

Example 1.10 Create an outline map of the US mainland

```
data usa_mainland; ❶
retain country 'USA'; ❷
set maps.us;
where state not in (2,15); ❸
run;

proc gremove ❹
data=usa_mainland
out=usa_outline
;
id state; ❺
by country;
run;

pattern v=me c=black;

title h=6 'US MAP DATA SET - NO INTERNAL BOUNDARIES';

proc gmap
map=usa_outline ❻
data=usa_outline
;
```

```
id country;
choro country / nolegend;
run;
quit;
```

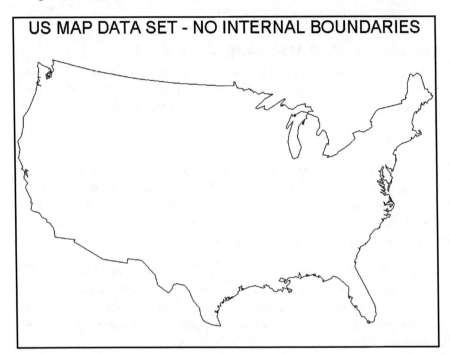

Figure 1.10 *Outline map of the US mainland (no Alaska or Hawaii)*

This example uses the US map data set to create a new map data set. ❶ A new variable, COUNTRY, is added to each observation in the new data set. ❷ The new variable will identify the new map areas for PROC GREMOVE. The map excludes observations for two states, Alaska (FIPS code 2) and Hawaii (FIPS code 15).❸ Two-character postal codes are probably more familiar than FIPS codes. You can use the FIPSTATE function to convert FIPS codes to two-character postal codes. You can use that function in the WHERE statement to exclude Alaska and Hawaii:

```
where fipstate(state) not in ('AK','HI');
```

The FIPSTATE function is used in subsequent examples when FIPS code specification is required.

PROC GREMOVE removes the state boundaries from the new data set. ❹ The variable that defines old map areas (STATE) is used as the ID variable, ❺ while the variable that defines the new map area (COUNTRY) is the BY variable. The new data set is used as both the map data set and the response data set. ❻ The map in Figure 1.10 depicts the outline of the continental United States.

1.4.2 PROC GPROJECT

Understanding the function of the GPROJECT procedure requires a little more knowledge of map data sets. The US map data set used to produce all the maps shown thus far contains projected X-Y coordinates—projected longitude and latitude, respectively—with Alaska and Hawaii repositioned at the lower right of the other states. The process of converting longitude and latitude from a spherical coordinate system to a flat, two-dimensional plane is called projection. PROC GPROJECT is used to convert the X-Y coordinates from latitude and longitude to arbitrary Cartesian coordinates. Referring to the X-Y coordinates in the US map data set as *projected* means that they have undergone this conversion process.

The map data set STATES also contains X-Y coordinates for state boundaries and contains the following variables:

VARIABLE	TYPE	LABEL
DENSITY	Num	Density for Lower Resolution Maps
SEGMENT	Num	State Segment Number
STATE	Num	State FIPS Code
X	Num	Unprojected Longitude in Radians
Y	Num	Unprojected Latitude in Radians

Although you can use both the US and STATES map data sets to create a map of the United States, there are two main differences between these data sets. First, the STATES data set contains an additional variable, DENSITY (more about that in the section on PROC GREDUCE). Next, the X-Y coordinates are unprojected. Figure 1.11 shows a map that results if the STATES data set is used directly with PROC GMAP. The following example substitutes STATES in the SAS code that produced Figure 1.1.

Example 1.11 Create a choropleth map using unprojected STATES map data set

```
proc format;
value pop
low      -< 1300000 = '<1.3'      1300000 -< 4000000 = '1.3-3.9'
4000000 -< 6000000 = '4.0-5.9'    6000000 -  high     = '6.0+'
;
run;

pattern1 v=ms c=grayfa; pattern2 v=ms c=grayda;
pattern3 v=ms c=grayaa; pattern4 v=ms c=gray5a;

title 'YEAR 2000 CENSUS POPULATION';

proc gmap
map=maps.states
data=us2000st
;
```

```
id state;
choro pop2000 / discrete coutline=black;
label pop2000 = 'MILLIONS';
format pop2000 pop.;
run;
quit;
```

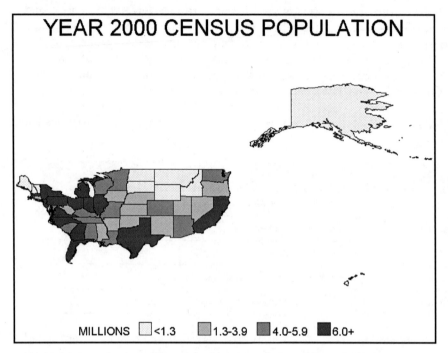

Figure 1.11 *Map created using unprojected STATES map data set*

There are several obvious differences between the map drawn with the projected US map data set and the map drawn with the unprojected STATES map data set. The unprojected map is drawn backwards and the shapes of all the map areas are distorted. Alaska and Hawaii are also now in approximately the correct position relative to the rest of the United States. The map areas face in the wrong direction since the X coordinate (longitude) in the map data set increases in size from east to west. PROC GMAP draws the map areas with an assumed origin in the lower-left corner and X coordinates increasing from left to right (west to east). The unprojected coordinates are measured on a sphere and have not been adjusted to fit on a flat surface. One difference that may not be obvious is the absence of Puerto Rico though the STATES map data set contains X-Y coordinates for Puerto Rico. Since the response data set did not provide a population for Puerto Rico, that map area was not drawn. This is the default behavior of PROC GMAP: it draws only map areas that correspond to map areas found in the response data set.

Before you can draw a map using a map data set with unprojected coordinates, the coordinates must be projected using PROC GPROJECT.

Example 1.12 Create a choropleth map drawn with projected STATES map data set

```
proc format;
value pop
low       -< 1300000 = '<1.3'
1300000 -< 4000000 = '1.3-3.9'
4000000 -< 6000000 = '4.0-5.9'
6000000 -  high     = '6.0+'
;
run;

proc gproject
data=maps.states ❶
out=projected_states ❷
;
id state; ❸
run;

pattern1 v=ms c=grayfa; pattern2 v=ms c=grayda;
pattern3 v=ms c=grayaa; pattern4 v=ms c=gray5a;

title 'YEAR 2000 CENSUS POPULATION';

proc gmap
map=projected_states ❹
data=us2000st
;
id state;
choro pop2000 / discrete coutline=black;
label pop2000 = 'MILLIONS';
format pop2000 pop.;
run;
quit;
```

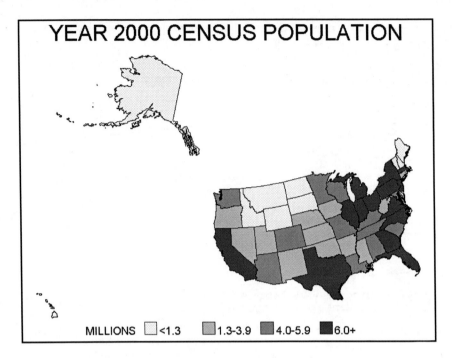

Figure 1.12 *Map drawn using projected STATES map data set*

PROC GPROJECT requires as input a map data set containing unprojected X-Y coordinates; in this example STATES is used. ❶ It creates a new map data set with projected coordinates. ❷ In addition to variables X and Y, the input data set must also contain a variable that associates each X-Y coordinate with a map area. This variable (STATE in the STATES data set) is used in the ID statement. ❸ The projected map data set is used in PROC GMAP ❹ to produce the map shown in Figure 1.12.

By default PROC GPROJECT expects the input data set to have the X-Y coordinates in radians and the X values to increase in value from east to west. All map data sets supplied by SAS that contain unprojected X-Y coordinates have these two features. Two options available in PROC GPROJECT can be used if a user-supplied map data set does not have either or both features: DEGREE, if coordinates are in degrees rather than radians; EASTLONG, if X values increase from west to east. A number of other options available in PROC GPROJECT are discussed in a later chapter.

You can exclude any areas that will not be displayed in the map by using a WHERE statement in PROC GPROJECT prior to using PROC GMAP.

Example 1.13 Create a projected STATES map excluding several areas

```
proc format;
value pop
low      -< 1300000 = '<1.3'
1300000 -< 4000000 = '1.3-3.9'
4000000 -< 6000000 = '4.0-5.9'
6000000 -  high     = '6.0+'
;
run;

proc gproject
data=maps.states
out=projected_states
;
where fipstate(state) not in ('AK','HI','PR'); ❶
id state;
run;

pattern1 v=ms c=grayfa;
pattern2 v=ms c=grayda;
pattern3 v=ms c=grayaa;
pattern4 v=ms c=gray5a;

title 'YEAR 2000 CENSUS POPULATION';

proc gmap
map=projected_states
data=us2000st
;
id state;
choro pop2000 / discrete coutline=black;
label pop2000 = 'MILLIONS';
format pop2000 pop.;
run;
quit;
```

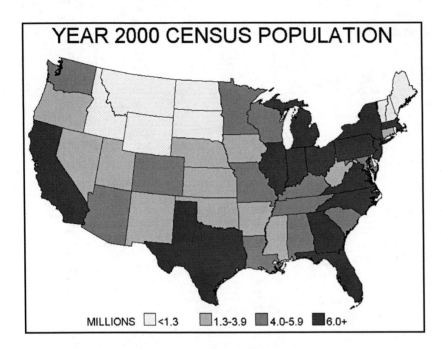

Figure 1.13 *Projected STATES map set (Alaska, Hawaii, and Puerto Rico excluded in PROC GPROJECT)*

This example uses a WHERE statement in PROC GPROJECT to exclude three map areas. ❶ The FIPSTATE function is used (as described after Example 1.10), allowing the states to be specified with two-character postal codes. AK, HI, and PR are the codes for Alaska, Hawaii, and Puerto Rico, respectively.

Map data sets supplied by SAS use two different terms to refer to unprojected X-Y coordinates, unprojected and deprojected. Although there are differences in the origins of the observations referred to by the different terms, map data sets with unprojected or deprojected observations should be treated the same—that is, the deprojected map data sets must also be projected with PROC GPROJECT prior to being used in PROC GMAP.

1.4.3 PROC GREDUCE

Several of the differences between the US and STATES map data sets have already been discussed, with emphasis on the difference between projected and unprojected X-Y coordinates. The two map data sets differ in two more respects. The STATES data set contains an additional variable, density, and it has over 50,000 observations while the US data set has just over 1,500. The large number of coordinates adds detail to maps drawn with the STATES map data set. Even on small maps, this enables you to see the extra detail along the coastlines and in the boundaries between the map areas. However, maps drawn with the US map data set, with only 1,500+ observations, look fine except for the omission of Long Island from New York State.

You can use PROC GREDUCE to add a density variable to map data sets. The density variable in the STATES map data set contains information about how much detail a given observation (X-Y coordinate) contributes to a map drawn using the data set. The procedure assesses how important each X-Y coordinate is in maintaining the original shape of map areas. The density variable can be used to reduce the complexity of map boundaries by eliminating those observations containing X-Y coordinates that are nonessential—that is, observations whose elimination does not significantly alter the appearance of the original map.

You can use PROC FREQ to create a table showing the number of observations with various levels of the variable density in the STATES data set.

DENSITY FOR LOWER-RESOLUTION MAPS				
DENSITY	FREQUENCY	PERCENT	CUMULATIVE FREQUENCY	CUMULATIVE PERCENT
0	1268	2.41	1268	2.41
1	1901	3.61	3169	6.02
2	1969	3.74	5138	9.75
3	10250	19.46	15388	29.21
4	37294	70.79	52682	100.00

The higher the value of the density variable, the more detail a given point adds to map area boundaries and the less important that point is in maintaining the overall appearance of the original map.

Example 1.14 Create a projected states map excluding observations with a density of 3 or greater

```
proc format;
value pop
low      -< 1300000 = '<1.3'
1300000 -< 4000000 = '1.3-3.9'
4000000 -< 6000000 = '4.0-5.9'
6000000 -  high     = '6.0+'
;
run;

proc gproject
data=maps.states
out=projected_states
;
where fipstate(state) not in ('AK','HI','PR') and density le 2; ❶
id state;
run;
```

```
pattern1 v=ms c=grayfa;
pattern2 v=ms c=grayda;
pattern3 v=ms c=grayaa;
pattern4 v=ms c=gray5a;

title 'YEAR 2000 CENSUS POPULATION';

proc gmap
map=projected_states
data=us2000st
;
id state;
choro pop2000 / discrete coutline=black;
label pop2000 = 'MILLIONS';
format pop2000 pop.;
run;
quit;
```

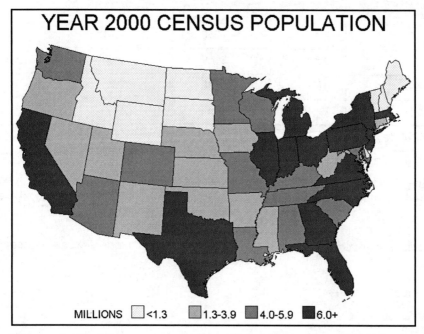

Figure 1.14 *Map created with limited observations from STATES map data set*

This example uses the WHERE statement in PROC GPROJECT to exclude three map areas (Alaska, Hawaii, and Puerto Rico), plus any observation with a density of three or greater.❶ Rather than using the FIPS codes for each state, this example uses the FIPSTATE function and postal codes (as was shown as an alternative method in Example 1.13). The map in Figure 1.14 looks similar to the map in Figure 1.13, though it was created using approximately

5,100 X-Y coordinates compared with the approximately 50,000 used for Figure 1.13. Using fewer observations allows maps to be drawn more quickly. If the output of PROC GMAP is being directed to a file rather than to the graph output window, maps drawn with fewer points require less storage space.

Not every map data set supplied by SAS contains a density variable. It is also unlikely that a user-supplied map data set would contain such a variable. PROC GREDUCE can be used to add a density variable to a map data set. This procedure requires a map data set as input and the specification of the variable within the data set that identifies map areas. PROC GREDUCE produces a new map data set that contains a density variable.

Example 1.15 Add a density variable to a map data set

```
proc greduce data=maps.mexico out=mexico_dens; ❶
id id; ❷
run;

proc freq data=mexico_dens; ❸
table density;
run;

pattern v=me c=black r=32; ❹
title h=6 "MAP CREATED WITH MEXICO MAP DATA SET";

proc gmap
map=mexico_dens ❺
data=mexico_dens
;
id id;
choro id / discrete nolegend;
where density le 4; ❻
run;
quit;
```

DENSITY	FREQUENCY	PERCENT	CUMULATIVE FREQUENCY	CUMULATIVE PERCENT
0	166	3.64	166	3.64
1	4	0.69	170	3.73
2	276	6.05	446	9.78
3	553	12.12	999	21.90
4	895	19.62	1894	41.53
5	952	20.87	2846	62.40
6	1715	37.60	4561	100.00

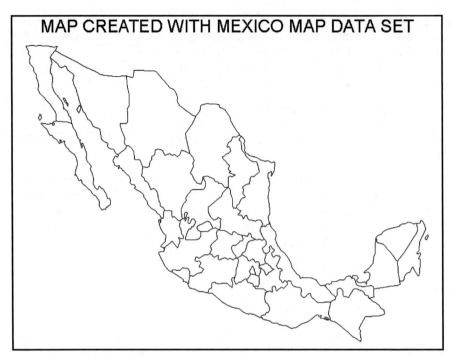

Figure 1.15 *Map created with limited observations after creating a density variable with PROC GREDUCE*

This example uses PROC GREDUCE to add a density variable to the MEXICO map data set, ❶ one of the map data sets supplied by SAS. The variable in the data set that identifies map areas is ID. ❷ A table of density values is created with PROC FREQ. ❸ The new variable can be used to reduce the number of observations used to create a map of Mexico. Thirty-two empty patterns are created, one for each map area in the Mexico map data set. ❹ The R= option specifies that the specified pattern be repeated 32 times. The new map data set, produced by PROC GREDUCE, is used to draw a map of Mexico, ❺ and a WHERE statement limits the observations used to draw the map to only those with a density of 4 or less ❻ (less than half the observations in the map data set).

Numerous options can be used in PROC GREDUCE. You can specify the maximum number of observations at various levels of the variable density using options N1 though N5 (the maximum number of points with a density of 1 through 5). Another set of options (E1 through E5) allows you to control the assignment of observations to various levels of density using a distance measure. The map in Figure 1.15 illustrates that using the default values of the various options can produce an acceptable map.

CHAPTER 2

Controlling the Appearance of Choropleth Maps

2.1 Chapter Overview

Four different types of maps were illustrated in Chapter 1. This and subsequent chapters are limited to one map type, choropleth. Though only choropleth maps are used in the examples, many of the concepts that are discussed are also applicable to the other map types. Most maps will need some explanatory text to augment the information contained in the display of map areas. This text can appear in titles, footnotes, and notes or can be part of a map legend. You can control the manner in which information is conveyed in the display of map areas by using PATTERN statements and the PROC GMAP options levels, midpoints, and discrete.

2.2 Titles, Footnotes, and Notes

TITLE, FOOTNOTE, and NOTE statements are used to add text to PROC GMAP output. These three statements have much in common: you can use the same options to alter the appearance of text added by any of the statements. However, the statements have several differences:

- Up to 10 TITLE and/or FOOTNOTE statements can be defined. There is no limit on the number of NOTE statements that can be defined.

- TITLE and FOOTNOTE statements are global and can appear anywhere within SAS code. NOTE statements are not global and must appear within a procedure.

- TITLE and FOOTNOTE statements are placed in their own areas within the graphics output. For this reason, they decrease the area available for any map drawn with PROC GMAP. Text added with a NOTE statement shares area with a map and does not affect map size. However, it is possible for text within a NOTE statement to write over a map. This overwriting will not occur with titles and footnotes.

The primary attributes of text added by any of the three statements are font, size, color, and location. Other attributes include angle (the angle of the baseline of the entire text string in relation to the map display) and rotation (the orientation of characters with respect to the baseline of the text string).

2.2.1 Fonts

Fonts may be specified using either the FTEXT= or FTITLE= option in a GOPTIONS statement or the FONT=option in a TITLE, FOOTNOTE, or NOTE statement. If no font is specified, the default font for TITLE1 is SWISS (similar to more familiar font names, such as Arial or Helvetica). The font for all other text in PROC GMAP is device dependent—it varies according to the device on which the map is displayed.

A number of fonts are supplied by SAS. They are software fonts, meaning that they are generated by PROC GMAP when creating graphics output. As such, they are available on any output device. In addition to plain text fonts, SAS supplies several fonts that contain special characters such as circles, squares, triangles, and stars that are useful in adding markers to maps, such as the location of a city.

Depending on the platform on which SAS is being used and the chosen output device, other fonts may be available. If you are running SAS in the Windows environment, you can use TrueType fonts. SAS/GRAPH can also make use of hardware fonts—that is, fonts that are native to the output device. One example is creating graphics on PostScript printers. These printers contain a standard collection of fonts that you can access by using statements such as

```
title1 font=hwps1009 'HELVETICA - POSTSCRIPT FONT';
title2 font=hwps1026 'HELVETICA NARROW - POSTSCRIPT FONT';
```

The naming scheme for hardware fonts is device specific, always starting with HW. Either two or three characters follow based on the module name for the device. If the module name is seven characters long, the last two characters are used. If the module name is eight characters long, the last three characters are used. Hardware font names end with a three-digit number, corresponding to the Chartype values (padded with leading zeros) defined for the device. The module names and Chartype numbers that correspond to the different fonts on a given output device can be found by using PROC GDEVICE:

```
* specify the catalog that contains the description of SAS-supported output devices;
proc gdevice c=sashelp.devices nofs;
* specify an output device - in this case PS, PostScript;
list ps;
quit;
```

Starting with SAS Version 8, the names of hardware fonts can also be used, as in the following example:

```
title1 font='Helvetica'         'HELVETICA - POSTSCRIPT FONT';
title2 font='Helvetica Narrow' 'HELVETICA NARROW - POSTSCRIPT FONT';
```

An easy way to see what any font looks like is to use PROC GSLIDE. This procedure requires no data set and will display all the text specified in any TITLE, FOOTNOTE, or NOTE statement(s).

Example 2.1 Display software and Truetype fonts using PROC GSLIDE

```
goptions htext=8 gunit=pct;
title1  font=swiss         'SWISS FONT'; ❶
title2  f=swissb           'SWISS BOLD FONT';
title3  f=swissi           'SWISS ITALIC FONT';
title4  f='Arial'          'ARIAL FONT'; ❷
title5  f='Arial/bo'       'ARIAL BOLD FONT';
title6  f='Arial/it'       'ARIAL ITALIC FONT';
title7  f='Arial Narrow' 'ARIAL NARROW';
title8;
title9  f='Arial' 'MARKER FONT: '    f=marker  'A B C D S U V'; ❸
title10 f='Arial' 'SPECIAL FONT:  ' f=special 'J K L M';
proc gslide; ❹
run;
quit;
```

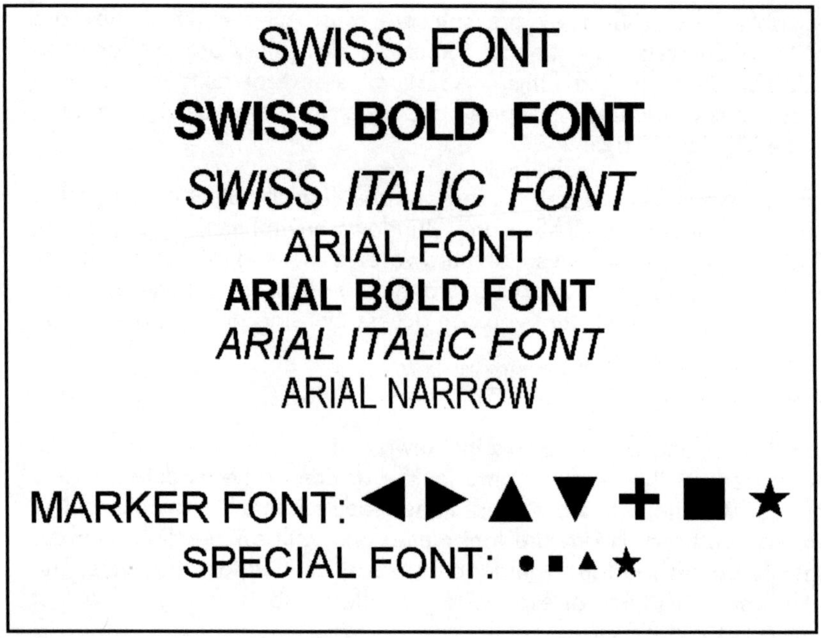

SWISS FONT

SWISS BOLD FONT

SWISS ITALIC FONT

ARIAL FONT

ARIAL BOLD FONT

ARIAL ITALIC FONT

ARIAL NARROW

MARKER FONT: ◀ ▶ ▲ ▼ ✚ ■ ★

SPECIAL FONT: ● ■ ▲ ★

Figure 2.1 *Software and TrueType fonts*

Figure 2.1 shows standard SAS software fonts ❶ as well as several variations of the Arial TrueType font. ❷ When using hardware fonts (such as TrueType fonts), you must enclose the font name in quotes. The case of the font name must match the case of the font as it appears in the given operating environment. Font attributes such as bold or italic are added following a slash placed after the font name. In Example 2.1, 'bo' specifies an attribute of the Arial font. There is no slash in the Arial Narrow font name since 'Narrow' is not an attribute of the Arial font; Arial Narrow is a full font name. Several characters are shown from the Marker and Special fonts. ❸ These characters are useful in specifying locations of features on maps. PROC GSLIDE is used to write the titles to the output device.

In Example 2.1, various keyboard characters produced a variety of symbols from the Marker and Special fonts. You can use PROC GFONT to display the keyboard characters or hexadecimal values that generate symbols for a given font.

```
title 'MARKER FONT';
proc gfont name=marker showroman nobuild;
run;
quit;

title 'SWISS FONT';
proc gfont name=swiss showroman romhex nobuild;
run;
quit;
```

For more information about PROC GFONT, see Example 4.3.

2.2.2 Size

You can control the size of text by using either the HTEXT= or HTITLE= option in a GOPTIONS statement or the HEIGHT= option in a TITLE, FOOTNOTE, or NOTE statement. If no heights are specified, the default size of the first title is two, while all other text will have a size of one. The actual height of text with a size of one, two, or any specified height is a function of the units specified for height of text. You can control the units for height by using a GUNIT= option in a GOPTIONS statement or by following the specification of height in the GOPTIONS statement or in a TITLE, FOOTNOTE, or NOTE statement. If no units for height are specified, the actual size of text is device dependent and is controlled by the number of character cells available on the output device.

The graphics output area for each output device supported by SAS/GRAPH is like a graphical spreadsheet, divided into character cells, where the number of cells is determined by the number of rows and columns available within the output area. The default number of rows and columns available for any device can be found using PROC GTESTIT:

```
proc gtestit pic=1;
run;
```

The output produced by PROC GTESTIT contains two numbers labeled R and C, showing the number of rows and columns, respectively. If the number of rows is 40, text with a height of one would occupy 1/40th of the vertical dimension of the output area. The number of rows and columns can also be determined without producing any graphical output. The following code displays the information in the SAS log:

```
goptions nodisplay;
proc gtestit;
run;
```

Rather than rely on the number of character cells to define units of text height, you can express units of text height in any of four other dimensions: IN, inches; CM, centimeters; PT, points (a point is 1/72nd of an inch); and PCT, percentage of the height of the graphics output area. One advantage of using PCT as the unit for text height is that text will have the same height relative to the height of the output area even when switching from one output device to another.

Example 2.2 Draw text at varying percentage of output area

```
goptions gunit=pct ftext='Arial';  ❶

title1  h=2   'TITLE1 H=2 PCT';  ❷
title2  h=4   'TITLE2 H=4 PCT';
title3  h=6   'TITLE3 H=6 PCT';
title4  h=8   'TITLE4 H=8 PCT';
title5  h=10  'TITLE5 H=10 PCT';
title6  h=12  'TITLE6 H=12 PCT';
title7  h=14  'TITLE7 H=14 PCT';
title8  h=16  'TITLE8 H=16 PCT';
title9  h=18  'TITLE9 H=18 PCT';
proc gslide;
run;
quit;
```

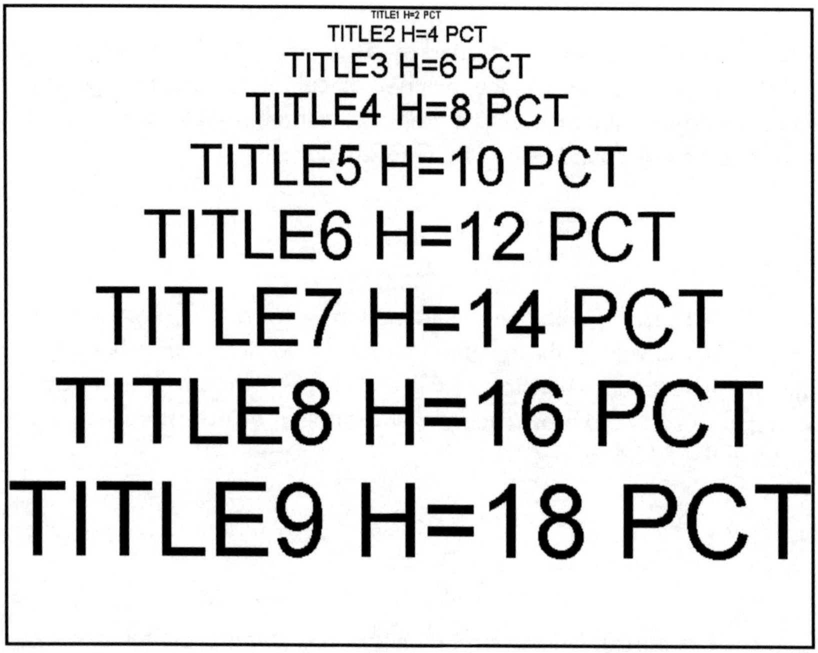

Figure 2.2 *Text drawn at varying heights with Arial font*

Both the default unit for text height and the font for text appearance are specified in a GOPTIONS statement. ❶ All text height will be considered as a percentage of the output area. The nine titles show how text looks drawn at varying heights. ❷ If any title, footnote, or note text is too big as specified to fit on a single line, SAS/GRAPH shrinks the text to fit on one line.

2.2.3 Color

Text color is a function of both the output device being used and SAS/GRAPH software. A default color list is associated with all output devices. If you request a text color that is not available for a given output destination, SAS/GRAPH remaps the color to one that is close to that specified or to the next available color in the color list. You can use PROC GDEVICE or PROC GTESTIT to display the color lists, with GTESTIT producing a test picture displaying colors. The default color list for color PostScript can be displayed using

```
proc gdevice c=sashelp.devices nofs;
list pscolor;
quit;
```

or

```
goptions dev=pscolor nodisplay;
proc gtestit pic=1;
run;
```

You can override the default color list in several ways: by specifying a color list in a GOPTIONS statement, using COLORS=(...); by using either the CTEXT= or CTITLE= option in a GOPTIONS statement to select a default color for all titles, footnotes, and notes; and by specifying colors within a TITLE, FOOTNOTE, or NOTE statement, using the COLOR= option. If both CTEXT= and CTITLE= options are used in a GOPTIONS statement, the color specified in CTITLE= will be used for titles, footnotes, and notes. Color naming schemes are discussed in Section 2.3, "Patterns."

2.2.4 Location

Titles, footnotes, and notes each have a different default location. Titles are placed at the top of the graphics output area, while footnotes are placed at the bottom of that area. Both titles and footnotes are centered by default. Notes are placed within the procedure output area, left-justified at the top. The location of text added by any of these statements can be changed using statement options.

Example 2.3 Change text location with justification and movement options

```
goptions gunit=pct htext=5 htitle=8 ftext='Arial'; ❶

title1     'TITLE1 CENTERED (DEFAULT)'; ❷
title2 j=l 'TITLE2 LEFT-JUSTIFIED';
title3 j=r 'TITLE3 RIGHT-JUSTIFIED';
footnote1     'FOOTNOTE1 CENTERED (DEFAULT)'; ❸
footnote2 j=l 'FOOTNOTE2 LEFT-JUSTIFIED'
          j=r 'FOOTNOTE2 RIGHT-JUSTIFIED';
```

```
proc gslide;
note      'NOTE LEFT-JUSTIFIED (DEFAULT)' ❹
    j=l 'NOTE LEFT-JUSTIFIED, NEW LINE CAUSED BY ANOTHER J=L' ❺
    move=(7,50)    'NOTE STARTED USING ABSOLUTE MOVE=(7,50)'
    move=(7,-20)   'NOTE STARTED USING RELATIVE MOVE=(7,-20)'
    move=(-65,-10) 'NOTE STARTED USING RELATIVE MOVE=(-65,-10)';
note 'NEW NOTE STATEMENT'; ❻
run;
quit;
```

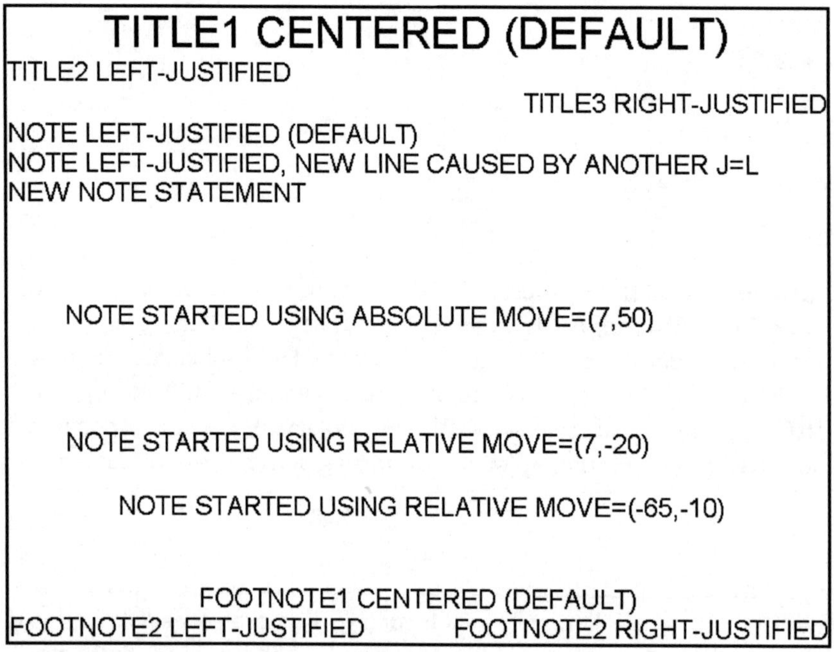

Figure 2.3 *Text placed at default and selected locations*

Two ways of controlling the location of text are justification (LEFT, CENTER, RIGHT) and movement to various locations within the output area. In this example you use a GOPTIONS statement to select default text heights and a font. ❶ The first title is drawn at the default location, centered and at the top of the output area. ❷ Two more titles are added; one is left-justified (using the J=L option), while the other is right-justified (using the J=R option). Since the two extra titles are added with separate statements, they occur on different lines. The first footnote is drawn at the default location, centered and at the bottom of the output area. ❸ Another footnote statement adds both left- and right-justified footnotes. Since both these footnotes are added with the same statement, they appear on the same line. Text added with the last footnote is at the very bottom of the output area.

NOTE statements are added within the procedure output area. ❹ The first note is at the default position, left-justified and at the top—that is, in the first available space after the titles have been placed in the output. More text is added with the same NOTE statement, with the position of the beginning of the text determined with several MOVE options. ❺ Specifying left justification with J=L results in the text being written on a new line. No units are specified in the MOVE options, so the coordinates default to the units specified in the GOPTIONS statement, percent of output area. The first move is to 7% in the X direction and 50% in the Y direction. The next move starts at the same X coordinate, but uses a plus sign preceding the Y coordinate, specifying a move relative to the last Y position. The last move specifies two relative coordinates. The starting Y position is again relative to the last Y position. The X location is relative to where the last added text ended, not relative to the position X=7% where it started. Another NOTE statement adds more text. ❻ Since this is a new statement, the position of the text reverts to the left side of the output area, just after any text added by the preceding NOTE statement excluding that added using any MOVE options.

2.2.5 Other Text Options

You can use several additional options to alter the appearance of text added with titles, notes, and footnotes. Two of these are ANGLE and ROTATE. The ANGLE option angles the baseline on which text is drawn, while the ROTATE option rotates text in relation to the baseline. Positive values for these options result in counterclockwise baseline movement and text orientation. There are differences in the effects of using the angles 90, −90, 270, and −270.

If a title is drawn at an angle of 90 or −270 degrees, it appears on the left of the graphics output area and is read from the bottom of the area to the top. The baseline of the text is parallel to the sides of the output. Drawing the titles at an angle of −90 or 270 degrees places text on the right of the graphics output area, and the text is read from the top of the area to the bottom. Once again, the baseline of the title is parallel to the sides of the output.

You can think of the effect of these angles on titles as drawing titles in the normal fashion at the top of a page, then rotating that page 90 degrees to the left (angle of 90 or −270 degrees) or to the right (angle of −90 or 270 degrees). The result of drawing a footnote at an angle of 90, −90, 270, or −270 can be understood in the same manner. Since footnotes normally appear at the bottom of the graphics output area, a footnote drawn at an angle of 90 or −270 degrees will appear on the right of the graphics output area, reading from bottom to top (again, think of a footnote at the bottom of a page, then rotate the entire page). When drawn at an angle of −90 or 270 degrees, footnotes appear on the left, reading from top to bottom.

Notes behave like titles when drawn at angles of 90, –90, 270, or –270 degrees. The only difference is that notes appear in the procedure output area rather than in the graphics area.

Example 2.4 Change text angle and rotation

```
goptions gunit=pct htext=5 ftext='Arial'; ❶

title1 angle=-10   'TITLE1 ANGLE=-10'; ❷
title2 angle=90    'TITLE2 ANGLE=90';
title3             'TITLE3 NO ANGLE SPECIFIED';
title4 angle=10    'TITLE4 ANGLE=10';
title5 angle=90;
title6 a=90 r=270 'TITLE6 A=90 R=270';
title7 angle=-90   'TITLE7 ANGLE=-90';
title8 angle=-90;
title9 a=-90 r=90 'TITLE9 A=90 R=90';

footnote1 angle=90    'FOOTNOTE1 ANGLE=90'; ❸
footnote2 angle=90;
footnote3 a=90 r=270 'FOOTNOTE3 A=90 R=270';
footnote4 angle=90;
footnote5 angle=-90   'FOOTNOTE5 ANGLE=-90';
footnote6 angle=-90;
footnote7 a=-90 r=90 'FOOTNOTE7 A=90 R=90';
footnote8 angle=-90;

proc gslide;
note angle=90 'NOTE ANGLE=90'; ❹
note angle=-90 'NOTE ANGLE=-90';
run;
quit;
```

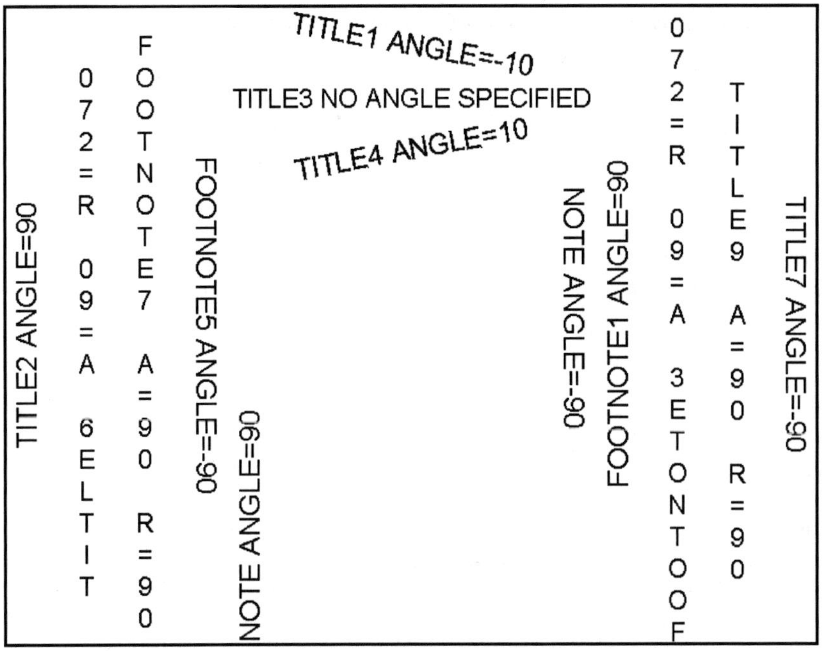

Figure 2.4 *Text with various angles and rotations*

This example uses a GOPTIONS statement to specify default text height and font. ❶ Titles are added at a variety of angles and rotations. ❷ The first title is at the default position, centered at the top of the output area, but at an angle of –10 degrees. The second title, with an angle of 90 degrees, appears at the left side of the output area, with text read from bottom to top. Since no angle is specified for the third title, it appears centered and just after TITLE1. The fourth title, drawn with the baseline at 10 degrees, appears centered in the output area, just after TITLE3. Titles five and six are both drawn at a 90 degree angle and are added just after the text from TITLE2, the last title drawn at a 90 degree angle. Title five just adds some blank space between titles two and six. A rotate option is used in TITLE6 to rotate the text 270 degrees. Titles seven through nine are drawn with a baseline angle of –90 degrees and appear on the right side of the output area.

Footnotes are also added with angles and rotations similar to those used in the TITLE statements. ❸ The 90 and –90 degree angles have the opposite effect on footnotes. An angle of 90 degrees puts a footnote on the right side of the output area. If no other text had already been drawn, FOOTNOTE1 would be at the right edge of the output area.

Notes are also added. ❹ Both notes are within the procedure output area. The 90 and –90 degree angle options have the same effect on text added with notes as they did on titles.

You can use other options to draw a box around text (BOX=) and to specify that any text will take precedence over procedure output (BLANK=). These options are not discussed here, but both are used in Example 3.5.

2.3 Patterns

The choropleth map examples in Chapter 1 used PATTERN statements to control the characteristics of the fill pattern used for map areas. If you do not use PATTERN statements, the patterns would be software-selected, with both the colors and styles dependent on the number of distinct patterns needed to distinguish among map areas.

Though patterns have only two attributes, VALUE and COLOR, there is a large variety of levels for each attribute, leaving many choices for either user-selected or software-selected patterns.

The fill for patterns is chosen with the VALUE= (or V=) option. The value can be solid (V=MS), empty (V=ME), or hatched. The hatching has three options: line density, style (parallel or crosshatched), and angle.

Example 2.5 Use PROC GMAP to show hatching patterns

```
goptions ftext='Arial' htext=4 gunit=pct cpattern=black;  ❶

data hatching;
input area x y @@;  ❷
datalines;
1 0 0   1 1 0   1 1 1   1 0 1   3 1 0   3 2 0   3 2 1   3 1 1
5 0 1   5 1 1   5 1 2   5 0 2   7 1 1   7 2 1   7 2 2   7 1 2
2 2 0   2 3 0   2 3 1   2 2 1   4 3 0   4 4 0   4 4 1   4 3 1
6 2 1   6 3 1   6 3 2   6 2 2   8 3 1   8 4 1   8 4 2   8 3 2
;
run;

pattern1 v=m1n0; pattern2 v=m1n45; pattern3 v=m1x0; pattern4 v=m1x45;  ❸
pattern5 v=m3n0; pattern6 v=m3n45; pattern7 v=m3x0; pattern8 v=m3x45;

proc gmap map=hatching data=hatching;  ❹
id area;
choro area / discrete;
label area='PATTERN #';
run;
quit;
```

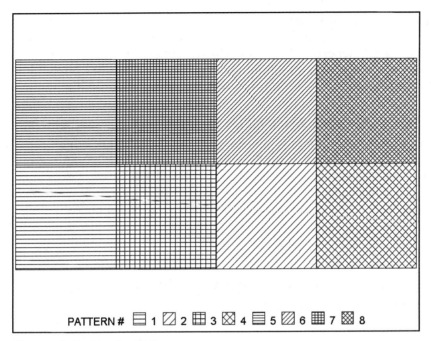

PATTERN # 1 2 3 4 5 6 7 8

Figure 2.5 *Hatched fill patterns*

The example uses a GOPTIONS statement to select a font, text height, and color for all patterns (CPATTERN=). ❶ A DATA step creates a map data set. ❷ Eight map areas are defined, all rectangles. PATTERN statements create eight patterns, one for each map area. ❸ The naming conventions for map hatching patterns are as follows: always begin with the letter M; specify the line density, ranging from 1 (lowest) to 5 (highest); specify either N for lines in one direction or X for cross-hatching; specify the angle of the lines. PROC GMAP is used to draw the filled rectangles.

No hatching patterns were used to draw any of the choropleth maps in Chapter 1. All PATTERN statements specified a solid fill, V=MS, and all map areas were identified by color defined by the gray scale; for example, COLOR=GRAY5A produced a dark gray. Color names can be expressed in six different ways. (Refer to the *SAS/GRAPH Software Reference* for a full discussion of color naming schemes.) Three common naming conventions are gray scale, RGB (red, green, blue), and the predefined color list for any given output device.

Gray-scale colors range from GRAY00 (black, or no color) to GRAYFF (white, or all colors combined). The numeric suffix is the hexadecimal representation of the numbers 0 through 255. For example, GRAY80 is halfway between black and white since a hexadecimal 80 is 128, or halfway between 0 and 255. Hexadecimal suffixes are also used to name RGB colors; the color names start with CX, followed by the amount or red, green, and blue in the color expressed as three hexadecimal pairs. For example, blue is named CX0000FF (00-no red, 00-no green, FF-all blue). Appendix A6 contains a SAS program that produces a mapping of the range of gray-scale colors, each labeled with the hexadecimal number used to create any given shade of gray. Appendix A6 also contains a program that produces a mapping of a range of colors, starting with a selected light color and progressing through a gradual darkening of that same color. Color lists are discussed in section 2.2.3.

2.4 DISCRETE, LEVELS, and MIDPOINTS Options

There are three options that control the number of different patterns used to distinguish among areas in a choropleth map. All are options in the CHORO statement in PROC GMAP. The DISCRETE option specifies that the response variable (the variable whose values are being mapped) be treated as a discrete rather than a continuous variable. Example 1.1 used a format to group map areas into four population ranges. The format was used in PROC GMAP together with the DISCRETE option:

```
choro pop2000 / discrete;
format pop2000 pop.;
```

Whenever your map formatted values of a response variable, you should use the DISCRETE option. Without it, the format will not group the response variable into the number of levels in the format, and PROC GMAP will choose the number of different levels of the response variable that are depicted in the map.

The block map in Example 1.6 used the LEVELS option instead of the DISCRETE option. In that map, the LEVELS option controlled the number of distinct heights for the blocks. When used with a choropleth map, the LEVELS options controls the number of different levels of the response variable that are mapped, and a different pattern is used for each level.

Example 2.6 Create a choropleth map using the LEVELS option

```
%macro pattern;❶
%do j=1 %to 48;
    %let i=%eval(255 - 4*&j);
    %let g=%sysfunc(putn(&i,hex2.));
    pattern&j v=s c=gray&g;
%end;
%mend;

%pattern;

title1 'YEAR 2000 CENSUS POPULATION';
title2 '(DARKER AREAS HAVE HIGHER POPULATIONS)';

proc gmap
map=maps.us
data=us2000st
;
where fipstate(state) not in ('AK','HI','DC'); ❷
id state;
choro pop2000 / levels=48 coutline=white nolegend; ❸
run;
quit;
```

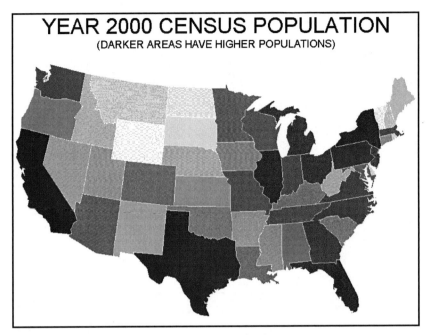

Figure 2.6 *Choropleth map drawn using the LEVELS option*

This example was a macro to create 48 PATTERN statements (the number of levels specified in PROC GMAP). ❶ The patterns will be colored with shades of gray, ranging from light gray to dark gray (GRAYFB through GRAY3B).

Two states (Alaska and Hawaii) and the District of Columbia are excluded from the map, ❷ resulting in 48 map areas to be displayed. A LEVELS option specifies the number of distinct levels of population to be displayed; the states are outlined in white, and the map legend is suppressed. ❸ When the intent of a map is just to show differences among map areas rather than exact values of the response variable, a choropleth map drawn with many levels of the response variable is a good choice. Remember, if the number of levels is not specified (and no DISCRETE or MIDPOINTS option is used), the number of levels is software-selected based on the range of the response variable.

You can use the MIDPOINTS option to specify a list of values of either a numeric or character response variable. There are several ways to specify numeric lists, including using exact values, using a starting and ending value with or without specifying an increment (assumed to be one if not specified), or using a combination of the two methods. When the response variable is a character variable, each midpoint value must be listed and the values listed in the MIDPOINTS option must match exactly the values of the response variable. The case of the value does not matter.

Example 2.7 Create a choropleth map using the MIDPOINTS option

```
pattern1 v=ms c=grayca;  ❶
pattern2 v=ms c=gray9a;
pattern3 v=ms c=gray6a;
pattern4 v=ms c=gray3a;

title 'US CENSUS BUREAU REGIONS';

proc gmap
map=maps.us
data=us2000st
;
id state;
choro region / midpoints='NORTHEAST' 'SOUTH' 'MIDWEST' 'WEST'
coutline=white;  ❷
label region="REGION";
run;
quit;
```

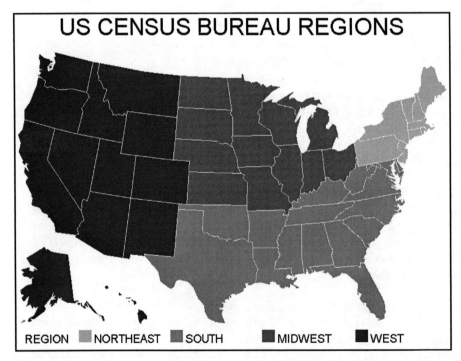

Figure 2.7 *Choropleth map drawn using the MIDPOINTS option*

The population data set US2000ST used in earlier examples contains a character variable, REGION, that places each observation in one of four U.S. Census Bureau regions. ❶ Four patterns are created to fill states in each of the four regions. The four midpoints are listed as part of the MIDPOINTS option, and the map areas are outlined in white using the COUTLINE= option. ❷

2.5 Legends

When you create a choropleth map, the map legend relates the patterns used to fill map areas to values of the response variable. By default the map legend is centered at the bottom of the output area. If the default legend location is used, the space occupied by the legend is affected in the same way as the space occupied by titles and footnotes—that is, the legend space decreases by the amount of space available to draw a map. If any footnotes are present, the legend is placed above the footnotes. PROC GMAP places a legend on all choropleth maps unless the legend is suppressed by the NOLEGEND option, as shown in Example 2.6. There will be one legend entry for each level of the response variable displayed in the map. If the legend had not been suppressed in Example 2.6, there would be 48 shaded boxes below the map, one for each of the 48 levels of the response variable (the populations of 48 states).

Legends have a number of attributes, some of which are location; appearance and content of text; and shape, size, and orientation of bars. You can change these attributes using a LEGEND statement. The statement itself does not create a legend. It merely creates a set of rules for the legend that is drawn when PROC GMAP is run with the LEGEND option.

Note: All the maps with legends shown thus far have actually used a LEGEND statement to alter one property, the shape of legend bars. No LEGEND statements were shown in the SAS code associated with each figure, reserving the discussion of legend attributes for this section.

Example 2.8 Use a LEGEND statement to alter the default legend attributes

```
pattern1 v=ms c=grayca;
pattern2 v=ms c=gray9a;
pattern3 v=ms c=gray6a;
pattern4 v=ms c=gray3a;

legend1 ❶
shape=bar(3,4) ❷
position=(top) ❸
label=none ❹
value=(font='Arial/it') ❺
frame ❻
fwidth=3 ❼
cshadow=gray9a ❽
;
```

```
title 'US CENSUS BUREAU REGIONS';

proc gmap
map=maps.us
data=us2000st
;
id state;
choro region / midpoints='NORTHEAST' 'SOUTH' 'MIDWEST' 'WEST'
               coutline=white legend=legend1;  ❾
run;
quit;
```

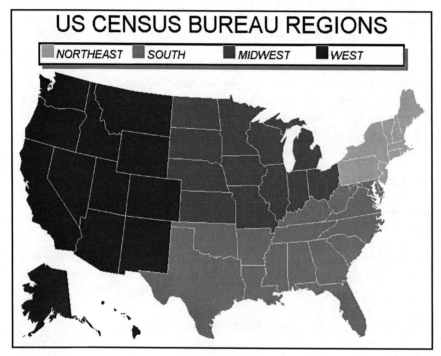

Figure 2.8 *Choropleth map with modified legend*

In this example, a LEGEND statement defines rules to alter the properties of a legend. ❶ The LEGEND statement is global and need not occur within any procedure. The name of the LEGEND statement in this example is LEGEND1, and this naming convention can be used to create up to 99 legends (LEGEND99). The first attribute changed is the shape of the shaded bars. ❷ Both X and Y dimensions are specified, but without any units. Units have been specified in the GOPTIONS statement—that is, GUNIT=PCT. Therefore, the size of the bars is 3% of the horizontal dimension and 4% of the vertical dimension. The specific combination of X and Y values needed to create square bars as shown in this example will vary depending on the units chosen and the output device being used to display PROC GMAP output. The

POSITION option moves the legend above the map. ❸ By default, a legend would appear above footnotes; when moved to the top, it appears below titles. Other position parameters allow the legend to be positioned either inside or outside the procedure output area. The default parameter is OUTSIDE. When you use the parameter INSIDE, the legend may appear on top of some of the map areas. The parameter for the default position is CENTER, but LEFT or RIGHT may also be chosen. The full description of the legend location in Example 2.8 is (TOP CENTER OUTSIDE).

The example uses a LABEL option to suppress the legend label. ❹ Since the title already explains that the shaded areas are regions, no label is needed. If a label is desired, the default label would be the name of the response variable (or its label if a label was associated with the response variable). You can specify a new label using the LABEL option, together with the label font, size, and orientation. The appearance of the text used to label the legend bars is changed with a VALUE option. ❺ The Arial Italic font supersedes the Arial font specified in the GOPTIONS statement. No text height is selected, so text height reverts to that chosen in the GOPTIONS statement, 4% of the output area. The box drawn around the legend is a result of the FRAME option, ❻ and its width is increased using the FWIDTH option. ❼ Just as the effect of the SHAPE option on the bars is device specific, the visual effect of altering the frame width from its default value of one might also change if another output device is used. The last option, CSHADOW, adds a drop shadow to the box around the legend with a gray-scale color. ❽ PROC GMAP is instructed to use these various options when creating a legend by using a LEGEND= option. ❾ Without this option, the map would be drawn with the default legend attributes.

CHAPTER 3

Variations on Basic Choropleth Maps

3.1   Chapter Overview

Options within both PROC GMAP and various SAS/GRAPH statements such as titles, patterns, and legends offer much flexibility in controlling the appearance of maps. These options, when combined with other SAS procedures and the power of the DATA step, further enhance the capabilities of PROC GMAP. A few of these capabilities have already been discussed (for example, outline maps and combining map areas were shown in Example 1.10). This chapter broadens the discussion by showing how to create a number of variations on basic choropleth maps.

3.2   Maps with Only Outlined Areas

Most choropleth maps shown thus far have had map areas with solid fills. There are a number of ways to produce a map with no shading and with only outlined map areas. A very simple method is shown in Example 3.1, using a map data set as both the map and the response data sets.

Example 3.1   Create an outline map using OBS=1

```
pattern1 v=me c=black;  ❶

proc gproject data=maps.states out=projected_states;
where fipstate(state) in ('ME','NH','VT','MA','RI','CT','NY');  ❷
id state;
run;

proc gmap map=projected_states data=projected_states (obs=1) all;  ❸
id state;
choro state / cempty=black nolegend;  ❹
note h=8 pct f='Arial/bo/it'
    'OUTLINE MAP' j=l 'OF NORTHEAST' j=l 'UNITED STATES';  ❺
run;
quit;
```

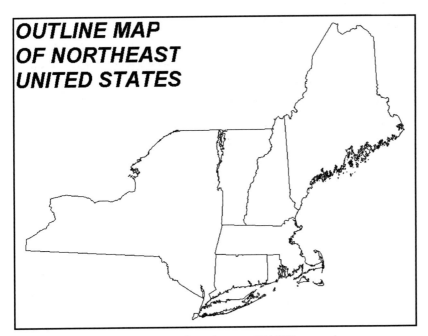

OUTLINE MAP OF NORTHEAST UNITED STATES

Figure 3.1 *Outline map produced using STATES map data set*

In this example, only one PATTERN statement is needed since the response data set in PROC GMAP uses only one observation. ❶ The unprojected STATES map data set is projected using PROC GMAP, and the content of the projected map is restricted to the seven northeastern states by using a WHERE statement. ❷ The projected map data set serves as both the map and response data sets. ❸ Only one observation is used from the response data set. The ALL option requests that PROC GMAP draw all map areas in the map data set. As was already mentioned in Chapter 1, the default action of PROC GMAP is to draw only those map areas present in the response data set. With a data set option of OBS=1 on the response data set, only one map area would be drawn without the ALL option. The CEMPTY= option specifies that empty map areas, those not matched to the response data set, are to be outlined in black, and the legend is suppressed. ❹ If another outline color was desired, the color would have to be changed in both the PATTERN statement and the CEMPTY= option.

The example uses a NOTE statement to add text to the map. ❺ The font is Arial Bold Italic. Notice that the map occupies the entire output area since there are no titles or footnotes and no legend. Notes begin in the upper left of the procedure output area and do not decrease the size of the map. The text is drawn on three lines by placing a text justification option (J=L) between the text sections. Since the default location is to start left-justified, each additional left-justification option results in a new line of text. If the first portion of the NOTE statement text had been preceded by J=R, additional right-justification commands would split the text over multiple lines.

3.3 Combining Map Areas into New Areas

In Figure 2.8, U.S. Census Bureau regions are shown using different gray-scale fills for regional map areas. The internal boundaries of all the states are still present in the map. There are also Census Bureau divisions within the larger regions. You can use the GREMOVE procedure to create a new map data set that contains just the outline areas of the divisions with no internal state boundaries.

Example 3.2 Create a map of census divisions—no internal state boundaries

```
* create a format ($STADIV) - used to assign states to census divisions;

proc format; ❶
value $sta2div
'CT','ME','MA','NH','RI','VT'                = 'NORTHEAST'
'NJ','NY','PA'                               = 'MID-ATLANTIC'
'IL','IN','MI','OH','WI'                      = 'EAST-NORTH-CENTRAL'
'IA','KS','MN','MO','NE','ND','SD'            = 'WEST-NORTH-CENTRAL'
'DE','DC','FL','GA','MD','NC','SC','VA','WV'  = 'SOUTH ATLANTIC'
'AL','KY','MS','TN'                          = 'EAST-SOUTH-CENTRAL'
'AR','LA','OK','TX'                          = 'WEST-SOUTH-CENTRAL'
'AZ','CO','ID','MT','NV','NM','UT','WY'       = 'MOUNTAIN'
'AK','CA','HI','OR','WA'                      = 'PACIFIC'
;
run;

* extract observations from the MAPS.STATES data set and add a new variable
* (DIVISION) using a PUT statement and the format $STADIV;

data states_divisions;
set maps.states;
where density le 3 and fipstate(state) not in ('AK','HI','PR');
division = put(fipstate(state),$sta2div.); ❷
run;

* sort the map data set by DIVISION;

proc sort data=states_divisions; ❸
by division;
run;

* use the GREMOVE procedure to remove the internal (STATE) boundaries from
* the new geographic areas, i.e. census divisions;

proc gremove data=states_divisions out=divisions; ❹
id state;
by division;
run;

* use the GPROJECT procedure to project the map data set;

proc gproject data=divisions out=divisions; ❺
id division;
run;

* select an empty pattern (ME) and repeat nine times, one per census
* division;

pattern1 v=me c=black r=9; ❻
```

```
* use the GMAP procedure to create a map of census divisions
* add descriptive text with a NOTE statement;

proc gmap map=divisions data=divisions; ❼
id division;
choro division / discrete nolegend;
note move=(2,3) pct h=4 pct f='Arial/bo/it' box=2
    'US CENSUS BUREAU DIVISIONS'; ❽
run;
quit;
```

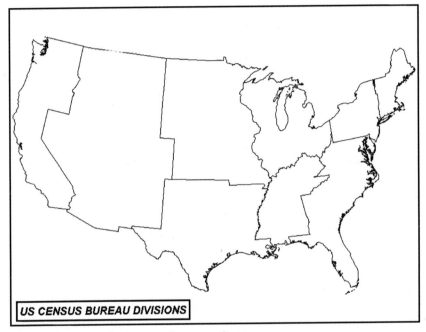

Figure 3.2 *Outline map of census divisions*

This example uses state postal codes to create a format that will convert a code to a census division. ❶ A new variable, DIVISION, is added to each observation in the STATES map data set using a PUT function and the FIPSTATE function. ❷ A new data set is created that excludes three map areas (Alaska, Hawaii, and Puerto Rico) and observations with extreme detail (density greater than 3, discussed in Section 1.4.3). The new data set is sorted by DIVISION, ❸ and PROC GREMOVE forms the new map areas (BY DIVISION) by combining old map areas (ID STATE). ❹ The new map is unprojected, so PROC GPROJECT is used. ❺ There are nine map areas, so nine empty patterns are created by using the repeat option (R=9) on one PATTERN statement. ❻ The new, projected map serves as both the map and response data sets. ❼ Text is added to the map with a NOTE statement, placed in the lower left of the output area using a MOVE option. ❽ A box is placed around the text using the BOX=2, where 2 specifies a moderately thick line.

3.4 Maps with Two ID Variables and Two Map Areas

Appendix A1.2 describes a data set (US2000CO) that contains both the 1990 and 2000 populations of each county in the United States. These data can be used to identify all the counties that had a population increase of 25% or more over the 10-year period. Once these counties are found, they can be displayed on a map. However, using PROC GMAP to display the location of these counties requires the use of two ID variables, STATE and COUNTY, to identify map areas. The map will display the boundaries of all state map areas and only those county map areas for counties with a 25% or higher increase in population. The map areas for both states and counties are found in map data set COUNTIES supplied by SAS.

Example 3.3 Create a map of counties with 25% or higher population increase, 1990 to 2000

```
* create a CNTLIN data set using only those observations from counties
* that had a 25% or higher population increase from 1990 to 2000;

data countyok (keep=fmtname start label); ❶
retain fmtname '$county' label 'OK';
set us2000co;
if (pop2000 - pop1990) / pop1990 ge .25;
start = put(state,z2.) || put(county,z3.);
run;

* use the FORMAT procedure and the CNTLIN data set to create the format
* $COUNTY;

proc format cntlin=countyok; ❷
run;

* extract observations from the MAPS.COUNTIES data set using a PUT statement
* and the format $COUNTY;

data counties; ❸
set maps.counties;
stcou = put(state,z2.) || put(county,z3.); ❹
if put(stcou,$county.) eq 'OK';
drop stcou;
run;

* combine observations from the MAPS.STATES data set (STATES boundaries)
* with observations that have been extracted from the MAPS.COUNTIES data set
* (COUNTIES)—exclude observations using a WHERE statement with postal codes
* and the DENSITY variable;
```

```
data state_county; ❺
set maps.states (in=from_states) counties;
where fipstate(state) not in ('AK','HI','PR') and density le 3;
if from_states then dummy=1; ❻
else                dummy=2;
run;

* use the GPROJECT procedure to project the combined state and county data
* set—use two ID variables, STATE and COUNTY;

proc gproject ❼
data=state_county
out=projected_counties
;
id state county; ❽
run;

* select a font for all text and specify that all heights are expressed in
* percentages of the graphics output area;

goptions ftext='Arial/it/bo' gunit=pct;

* select two patterns for map areas - an empty (ME) pattern for states and a
* solid (MS) pattern for counties;

pattern1 v=me c=black; ❾
pattern2 v=ms c=grayc8;

* add descriptive text to the map with TITLE and FOOTNOTE statements;

title1      h=6 'COUNTIES WITH 25+% INCREASE IN POPULATION';
title2      h=5 '1990 TO 2000';
footnote j=l h=4 'U.S. CENSUS BUREAU';

* use the GMAP procedure to create the map - use two ID variables, STATE and
* COUNTY;

proc gmap
map=projected_counties
data=projected_counties;
id state county; ❿
choro dummy / discrete coutline=black nolegend;
run;
quit;
```

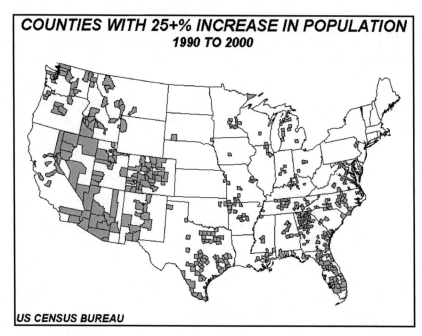

Figure 3.3 *Map with two ID variables, state and county*

The first DATA step in this example creates a CNTLIN data set, used in PROC FORMAT to create the $COUNTY format. ❶ The $COUNTY format is used in a later DATA step to select map areas from the county map data set that have increased in population by 25% or more from 1990 to 2000. Since county FIPS codes are repeated from state to state, both a state FIPS code and a county FIPS code are needed to identify any given county. The state and county FIPS codes are combined into a new variable, START, that will become part of the format used to select map areas. PROC FORMAT creates the format from the CNTLIN data set. ❷ Next, the format $COUNTY is used to create a data set that contains only those map areas from the COUNTIES map data set that match a county identified by the format. ❸ The STATE and COUNTY variables are combined into one variable, STCOU, and the value of that variable is checked to see if it appears as part of the format created earlier. ❹

A new map data set is created containing both state map areas and the selected county map areas. ❺ Three map areas are excluded (Alaska, Hawaii, Puerto Rico), and only observations with a density of three or less are kept in the data set. An IN= data set option is used to identify observations from the data set containing state map areas, and a new variable, DUMMY, with a value of 1 is added to each of these observations. ❻ The same variable is added to all other observations (the county map areas) with a value of 2. Values of the variable DUMMY and PATTERN statements will be used to control the fill of map areas. The map is projected ❼ and two map areas are specified using the ID statement. ❽ PATTERN statements define two patterns. ❾ The first pattern is empty and is used to create outlined states, while the second pattern specifies a gray-scale fill that is used to shade the counties.

PROC GMAP creates the map, and just as in PROC GROJECT, two variables are specified in the ID statement. ❿ The projected map data set is also used as the response data set and the variable DUMMY is mapped (with values of only 1 or 2). The map areas are outlined in black and the legend is suppressed.

3.5 Clipped Maps

Figure 3.1 is created by selecting several states from the STATES map set. The map shows the entire area of each state. Rather than showing entire map areas, there are two ways (PROC GPROJECT and PROC GREPLAY) to create clipped maps—that is, maps with map areas truncated along straight lines of latitude and/or longitude drawn through map areas.

3.5.1 Clipping Maps with PROC GPROJECT

You can clip unprojected maps using options in PROC GPROJECT. Clipping is done along lines of latitude and/or longitude and any or all of the following options may appear: LATMIN, LATMAX, LONGMIN, LONGMAX. Each of these options can be thought of as specifying one of the four sides of a box drawn around a map area. For map areas in the northern hemisphere, LATMIN selects the location of the lower side of the box while LATMAX selects the upper side. In the western hemisphere, LONGMIN and LONGMAX specify the location of the right and left sides of the box, respectively.

All options are expressed in degrees. The following example produces a map of the central United States clipped on four sides (bounded by the box defined using the four options just described).

Example 3.4 Clip a map with PROC GPROJECT

```
* select a font for all text and specify that all heights are expressed in
* percentages of the graphics output area;

goptions ftext='Arial/it/bo';

* use the GPROJECT procedure to both project the MAPS.STATES data set
* and clip the map at specified latitudes and longitudes;

proc gproject
data=maps.states
out=clipped_map
longmax=105 ❶
longmin=87
latmin=33
latmax=44;
id state;
run;

* add descriptive text with a TITLE statement;

title h=6 'MAP CLIPPED WITH PROC GPROJECT';
```

```
* select an empty (ME) pattern for map areas;

pattern v=me c=black;

* use the GMAP procedure to create the map from the clipped-projected data
* set;

proc gmap
data=clipped_map (obs=1)
map=clipped_map
all;
id state;
choro state / discrete cempty=black nolegend;
run;
quit;
```

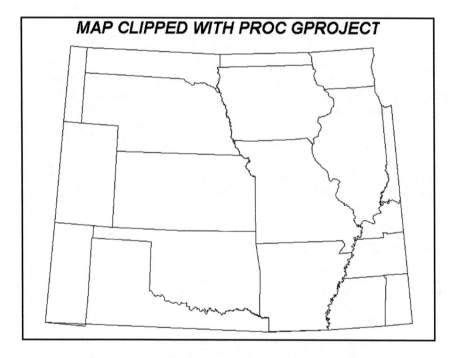

Figure 3.4 *Map clipped on four sides using PROC GPROJECT*

All four possible clipping options are used in PROC PROJECT. ❶ Since lines of longitude are farthest apart at the equator and get closer as they approach the poles, the clipping on both the left and right appears at an angle. Projection of lines of latitude from a spherical surface to a flat surface results in curved lines. Thus, the clipping at the top and bottom of the map appears curved. The smaller the area displayed, the smaller the angle in the lines of longitude and the less curvature in the lines of latitude.

3.5.2 Clipping Maps with PROC GREPLAY

You can use PROC GREPLAY to redisplay the output from PROC GMAP that is stored in a catalog. Each time PROC GMAP is used to produce a map, the output is directed to both the chosen output device and an entry in a graphics catalog. The default graphics catalog is named GSEG and is located in the WORK library. The names of the entries in the catalog are created by SAS/GRAPH and default to the name of the procedure that produces the entry, followed by a numeric suffix, such as GMAP1. The name of the graphics catalog can also be user selected (using a GOUT= option in the PROC GMAP statement), as can the names of the entries (using a NAME= option in the CHORO statement).

When entries are redisplayed, they are created in templates (not to be confused with ODS templates). A template is a set of rules that define a space in which to display the output from PROC GREPLAY. The rules comprise the coordinates of a polygon. In most cases, the polygon is a rectangle of a different size from the original output. All coordinates are expressed in percentages of the graphics output area. If PROC GMAP output is redisplayed in a rectangle whose lower-left corner is (0,0) and upper-right corner is (50,50), the entire map will be displayed as a space that is only one-quarter the size of the original map. However, if coordinates are used that are less than zero or greater than one hundred, the effect is to zoom in on an area of a map.

Example 3.5 Clip a map with PROC GREPLAY

```
* select a font for all text and specify that all heights are expressed in
* percentages of the graphics output area;

goptions ftext='Arial/it/bo' gunit=pct;

* use the GPROJECT procedure to project the MAPS.STATES data set
* exclude observations using a WHERE statement and postal codes;

proc gproject data=maps.states out=proj;  ❶
id state;
where fipstate(state) not in ('AK','HI','PR');
run;

* select an empty (ME) pattern for map areas;

pattern v=me c=black;  ❷

* use the GMAP procedure to create a map
* add the map to the graphics catalog "holdmaps" with the name "usa";

proc gmap
data=proj (obs=1)
map=proj
all
gout=holdmaps;  ❸
id state;
choro state / discrete cempty=black nolegend name='usa';  ❹
note move=(40,50) h=2 color=white box=1 blank=yes
                  color=black 'MAP CLIPPED WITH PROC GREPLAY';  ❺
run;
quit;
```

```
* use the GREPLAY procedure to create a clipped map by redrawing the map
* in an enlarged space, displaying only that portion that fits in the
* space ranging from 0 to 100 in both the X and Y direction;

proc greplay igout=holdmaps nofs; ❻
tc    template;
tdef tins 1/llx=-100 ulx=-100 lrx=200  urx=200 ❼
           lly=-100 uly=200  lry=-100 ury=200
;
template tins; ❽
tplay 1:usa;
quit;
```

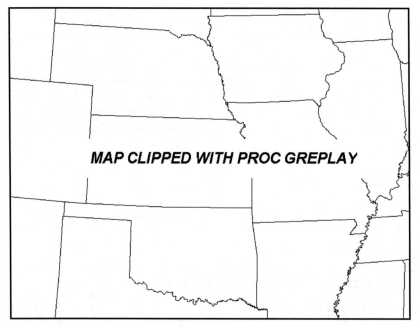

Figure 3.5 *Map clipped on four sides using PROC GREPLAY*

This example creates a projected map data set from the STATES map data set, excluding Alaska, Hawaii, and Puerto Rico. ❶ All map areas will be empty and outlined in black, using the technique described in section 3.2. ❷ An alternative (HOLDMAPS) to the default graphics catalog name (GSEG) is specified using the GOUT= option. ❸ The graphics entry placed in the HOLDMAPS catalog is named USA using the NAME= option. ❹ A note is added to the center of the map. ❺ The note will be drawn over a blank white background using several NOTE statement options: COLOR, BOX, and BLANK. PROC GREPLAY is used to redisplay the map, now stored in catalog HOLDMAPS as the entry USA using the IGOUT= option. ❻ The NOFS option specifies that the procedure will be run in line mode, not full-screen interactive mode. A template for redisplay of the map is defined, with coordinates that would make it larger than the original map. ❼ The map is expanded to fill the template range −100 to 200, but the display can use only the portion of the range from 0 to 100. Portions of the map falling outside the displayed range are clipped.

The specified coordinates will zoom in on the center of the map. The TEMPLATE and TPLAY commands replay the map in the newly defined template. ❽ The output in Figure 3.5 is similar to that shown in Figure 3.4, in which the map was clipped using PROC GPROJECT. Though similar, all map area boundaries now run to the edges of the map. The note appears in the center, with map area boundaries behind the note erased by the combination of the COLOR, BOX, and BLANK options.

3.6 Drawing a Map to Scale

The default behavior of PROC GMAP is to maximize the use of the procedure output area without introducing any distortion in the shape of map areas. Users can control the size of the map by including the YSIZE= and/or XSIZE= option in PROC GMAP. If only one option is used, PROC GMAP selects the other, again with the constraint of not distorting the shape of map areas. The YSIZE= option together with some information from a map data set enables the creation of a map with a set scale, such as one mile per inch.

Example 3.6 Create an outline map of northeast United States drawn to scale

```
* use the SUMMARY procedure to find the minimum and maximum latitude and
* longitude of seven northeastern states;

proc summary data=maps.states; ❶
var y;
where fipstate(state) in ('ME','NH','VT','MA','RI','CT','NY'); ❷
output out=stats (keep=max_lat min_lat)
       max=max_lat min=min_lat; ❸
run;

* compute the distance in miles between the minimum and maximum latitudes
* compute map height in inches - divide the distance in miles by 150
* the map will have a scale of 150 miles to the inch
* place that distance (now in inches) in a macro variable named &HEIGHT;

data _null_;
set stats;
range_miles = 3949.99 * (max_lat - min_lat); ❹
height      = range_miles / 150; ❺
call symput('height',put(height,10.2)); ❻
run;

* use the GPROJECT procedure to project the MAPS.STATES data set
* use a WHERE statement with postal codes to select nine northeastern states;
```

```
proc gproject
data=maps.states
out=projected_states
;
where fipstate(state) in ('ME' 'NH' 'VT' 'MA' 'RI' 'CT' 'NY'); ❼
id state;
run;
* select an empty (ME) pattern for map areas;

pattern v=me c=black;

* use the GMAP procedure to create the map
* specify map height using the YSIZE= option and the macro variable &HEIGHT
* add descriptive text with a NOTE statement;

proc gmap
map=projected_states
data=projected_states (obs=1)
all
;
id state;
choro state /  discrete ysize=&height in ❽
               cempty=black nolegend;
note h=6 pct f='Arial/bo/it'
          'OUTLINE MAP OF NORTHEAST UNITED STATES'
     j=l 'DRAWN TO SCALE:  1 INCH = 150 MILES';
run;
quit;
```

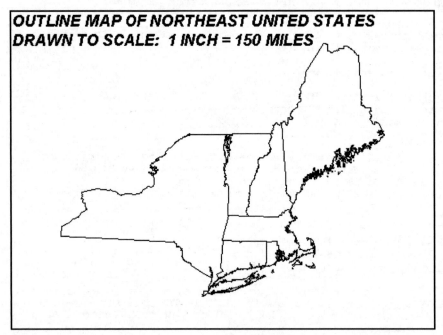

Figure 3.6 *Map drawn to scale using the PROC GMAP option YSIZE*

This example uses PROC SUMMARY to determine the minimum and maximum values of latitude in the map areas that are to be displayed using PROC GMAP. ❶ The STATES map data is used and map areas are restricted to the northeastern United States. ❷ A SAS data set (STATS) is created that contains one observation and two variables: MAX_LAT, the maximum latitude; and MIN_LAT, the minimum latitude. ❸ An approximate distance formula uses the polar radius of the earth in miles (3949.99) and the difference between the maximum and minimum latitudes found with PROC SUMMARY to calculate the north-south range of the map data set in miles. ❹ Note that this formula works with data from map data sets supplied by SAS since the X-Y coordinates in the map data sets are in radians. A scale of 150 miles to the inch is to be used, so the range in miles is divided by 150 to determine the vertical size of the map. ❺ The height is stored in a macro variable &HEIGHT, to be used later for control of map size in PROC GMAP. ❻ The STATES map data set is projected, restricting the map to states in the northeast United States. ❼ PROC GMAP is used to draw a map with a height specified by the YSIZE= option. ❽ The text stored earlier in the macro variable height is substituted in the procedure.

The map in Figure 3.6 is slightly smaller than the map of the same states shown in Figure 3.1. The map in Figure 3.1 was created under the default rule of maximum size with no map area distortion, while the map in Figure 3.6 had its height controlled by the YSIZE= option.

More Information

The technique of drawing a map to scale first appeared in "Drawing a Map to Scale," in *SAS Communications*, vol. 14, no. 3 (1989), 32-33. The SAS code in Example 3.6 is based on that article, which notes that this method is only an approximation and is most accurate when mapping relatively small areas.

3.7 Creating an Inset with PROC GREPLAY

When map areas are very small, they are difficult to see when displayed on a map together with large map areas. For example, though the District of Columbia is present on most of the United States maps shown thus far, it cannot be seen well. One way to display small map areas is to create an inset that zooms in on a specific portion of a larger map. Map insets can be displayed using PROC GREPLAY.

On a choropleth map displaying populations of New York State, the five counties comprising New York City are quite small and difficult to see. A map showing all New York State counties is drawn, with the New York City counties displayed in an inset. The response data set (NYS2000CO) used in this example is described in Appendix A1.3.

Example 3.7 Display small map areas in an inset

```
* select a font for all text and specify that all heights are expressed in
* percentages of the graphics output area;

goptions ftext='Arial/bo/it' htext=4 gunit=pct ;

* create a format (POP) to group states by population;

proc format; ❶
value pop
  low    -<   50000 = '<50'        50000 -<  100000 = '50-99'
100000 -<  500000 = '100-499'     500000 -   high   = '500+' ;
run;

* use the GPROJECT procedure twice, each time using a WHERE statement to
* select only New York state counties
* first, project the MAPS.COUNTIES data using all New York state counties
* second, project the MAPS.COUNTIES data set, but
* clip the map on three sides using latitude and longitude, creating a data
* set with projected X-Y coordinates of the New York City area;

proc gproject data=maps.counties out=nys; ❷
where fipstate(state) eq 'NY';
id county;
run;

proc gproject data=maps.counties out=nyc ❸
longmax=74.29
longmin=73.69
latmax=40.95
;
where fipstate(state) eq 'NY';
id county;
run;
* select solid patterns (MS) for map areas - fills are shades of gray;

pattern1 v=ms c=grayda; ❹
pattern2 v=ms c=grayaa;
pattern3 v=ms c=gray8a;
pattern4 v=ms c=gray5a;

* use a LEGEND statement to create a legend;

legend1 shape=bar(3,4) origin=(5,70) pct across=2 mode=share ❺
        label=(j=l position=top 'THOUSANDS');

* add descriptive text with a TITLE statement;

title h=5 'YEAR 2000 CENSUS POPULATION - NEW YORK STATE';

* use the GMAP procedure to create a map of all New York State counties
* add the map to the graphics catalog "holdmaps" with the name "NYS";

proc gmap map=nys data=nys2000co gout=holdmaps; ❻
id county;
choro pop2000 / discrete coutline=white legend=legend1 name='NYS';
note move=(62,6) pct box=1 h=2 'SEE INSET'; ❼
format pop2000 pop.;
run;
quit;

* clear the title and use a GOPTIONS statement to add a BORDER to subsequent
* maps;
```

```
title;
goptions border; ❽

* use the GMAP procedure to create a map of the clipped area
* add the map to the graphics catalog "holdmaps" with the name "NYC"
* add descriptive text with a NOTE statement, specify a HEIGHT of 10
* the large text will be reduced when displayed in an inset;

proc gmap map=nyc data=nys2000co gout=holdmaps; ❾
id county;
choro pop2000 / discrete coutline=white nolegend name='NYC';
format pop2000 pop.;
note h=10 ' NEW YORK CITY';
run;
quit;

* use the GREPLAY procedure to place two maps in the graphics output area
* replay the New York State map in the full output space
* replay the New York City map in a small area in a reduced output space;

proc greplay igout=holdmaps nofs; ❿
tc    template;
tdef tins 1/llx=0     ulx=0    lrx=100 urx=100
            lly=0     uly=100  lry=0    ury=100
          2/llx=30    ulx=30   lrx=55   urx=55
            lly=3     uly=28   lry=3    ury=28 ;
template tins;
tplay 1:nys 2:nyc;
quit;
```

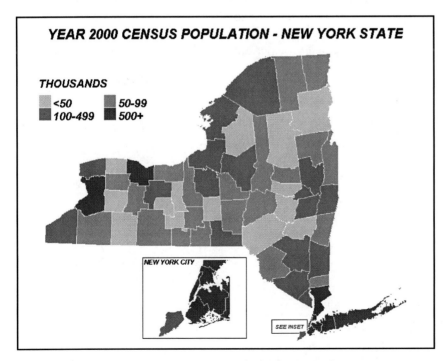

Figure 3.7 *Map with inset created with PROC GREPLAY*

This example creates a format that groups counties into four population-based groups. ❶ New York counties are extracted from the COUNTIES data set supplied by SAS and the counties are projected. ❷ To create the inset map, the COUNTIES data set is used again, but the projected map data set is clipped on three sides using PROC GPROJECT options. ❸ The clipped area is New York City, plus a small portion of two bordering counties. Approximate values of the variables LONGMAX, LONGMIN, and LATMAX used in PROC GPROJECT were determined using a map of New York State that displayed a grid of lines of longitude and latitude. The exact values were determined using a process of trial and error—that is, creating the clipped maps with different values until a suitable map was produced.

Patterns are defined to fill map areas, ❹ and a LEGEND statement defines the display of the map legend. ❺ Notice that the legend is moved to the upper-left portion of the output area using the ORIGIN option. The map of New York counties is created ❻ and the map output is stored in a graphics catalog (HOLDMAPS) in the WORK library with the name NYS. A note is added at the location of New York City with instructions to see the inset. ❼ Before creating the map of New York City counties, a TITLE statement blanks out the TITLE used in the statewide map and a GOPTIONS statement is used to create a border around the map to be used as an inset. ❽ The New York City map is created and the output is stored as an entry in the HOLDMAPS catalog. ❾ Since the map will be scaled down to fit below New York in the output area, the height of the note is increased (H=10) so it will be readable when the map is displayed. PROC GREPLAY is used to redisplay the two maps. ❿ The statewide map is displayed in a template that covers the entire output area, while the New York City map is displayed in an inset.

CHAPTER 4

Enhancing Choropleth Maps Using the Annotate Facility

4.1 Chapter Overview

The variations on basic choropleth maps shown in all the examples thus far have been created using SAS/GRAPH procedures and/or global statements such as TITLE, LEGEND, and PATTERN. Although the procedures and statements offer a wide variety of options, you cannot accomplish some tasks without resorting to another SAS/GRAPH feature, the annotate facility. You can make a wide variety of additions to a map with annotation. To use the annotate facility, first you create an Annotate data set that defines what is to be added to a map, where it will be placed, how it will appear, and when it will be added. You then apply annotation to the map using the ANNOTATE= option in PROC GMAP. Some of the common "whats" that can be added are labels that name geographic areas and symbols that mark the locations of cities or other entities. The "where" usually comprises X-Y coordinates in terms of longitude and latitude. There are many options associated with "how." If labels are being added, "how" includes the font, font size, and color. "When" has only two options, before or after the map is drawn.

4.2 Adding Labels to Map Areas

SAS supplies a data set (USCENTER) containing the location of the visual center of each state. For several states located in the northeast, the data set also contains an alternative location for a label, which is not at the state center but in the Atlantic Ocean. The variable OCEAN has a value of Y for all ocean locations and N for all true state centers.

Example 4.1 Add labels from USCENTER data set to a projected map data set

```
* create an Annotate data set (ADD_LABELS)
* extract information on location of the labels for seven northeastern
* states from the MAPS.USCENTER data set (the PROJECTED X-Y coordinates are
* used);

data add_labels; ❶
retain function  'label' ❷
       xsys ysys '2'
       position  '5'
       color     'black'
       style     '"Arial/bo/it"'
       size      3
       hsys      '3'
       cbox      'white'
       when      'a';
set maps.uscenter; ❸
where fipstate(state) in ('CT','ME','MA','NH','NY','RI','VT') and ocean ne
'Y'; ❹
text = fipname(state); ❺
run;

* select a solid (MS) pattern for map areas, repeat the pattern seven times;

pattern v=ms c=gray88 r=7; ❻
```

```
* use the GMAP procedure to create a map and add labels with an ANNOTATE=
* option—add descriptive text with a NOTE statement;

proc gmap
map=maps.us
data=maps.us;
where fipstate (state) in ('CT','ME','MA','NH','NY','RI','VT');
id state;
choro state / discrete coutline=white nolegend annotate=add_labels; ❼
note h=5 pct f='Arial/bo/it' 'MAP LABELS ON US MAP DATA SET';
run;
quit;
```

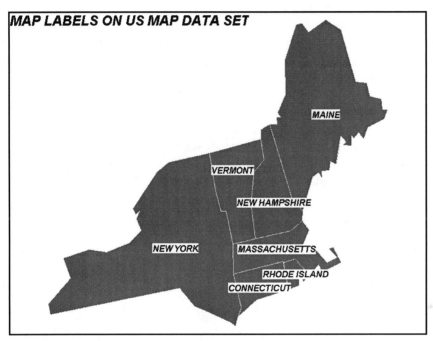

Figure 4.1 *Labels added to a projected map*

This example creates an Annotate data set with instructions that will add labels to map areas. ❶ A RETAIN statement assigns values to many of the variables that determine the "what," "where," "how," and "when" attributes of the data set. ❷

What   The first variable, FUNCTION, is "what" is to be added, a label.

Where   The next set of variables are part of "where": variables XSYS and YSYS with a value of 2 specify that the X-Y coordinates of map labels are in the same units as the map (graphics output), in this case longitude and latitude; a value of 5 for POSITION results in a label centered on the point set by the variables X and Y.

How   Another set of variables describes "how" the label will appear: COLOR, black; STYLE, font Arial Bold Italic; SIZE, height of 3, with units of percentage of output area (HSYS=3). A white box is placed behind each label, CBOX 'white', to make it easier to read the black labels on a dark background.

When   The labels are added after the map is drawn. WHEN is 'a' meaning "after" ('b' means "before").

The X-Y coordinates (another portion of "where") and state number are read from the USCENTER data set.❸ The labels are limited to those in the northeast, and all observations with X-Y locations in the ocean are discarded.❹ The FIPNAME function is used to create text (another portion of "what"), a state name from the state FIPS code.❺ Patterns are defined for the seven states, a solid gray.❻ The map is drawn with PROC GMAP and the annotation is added by using the ANNOTATE= option.❼

Both the US map data set and the USCENTER data set contain projected X-Y coordinates. The map shown in Figure 4.1, created using the US map data set, does not have the detail that can be seen in Figure 3.1, created using the STATES map data set. The STATES map data set and the USCENTER data set can be used to draw a labeled map with more detail, but the process is a bit more involved since the STATES data set is unprojected.

Example 4.2 Add labels from USCENTER data set to an unprojected map data set

```
* create an Annotate data set (TEMP_LABELS)
* extract information on location of the labels for seven northeastern
* states from the MAPS.USCENTER data set - select the UNPROJECTED X-Y
* coordinates LONG and LAT and convert them from degrees to radians;

data temp_labels; ❶
retain function  'label'
       xsys ysys '2'
       position  '5'
       color     'black'
       style     '"Arial/bo/it"'
       size      3
       hsys      '3'
       when      'a'
       cbox      'white';
set maps.uscenter;
where fipstate (state) in ('CT','ME','MA','NH','NY','RI','VT') and ocean ne
'Y';
x = long * constant('pi') / 180; ❷
y = lat  * constant('pi') / 180;
text = fipname(state);
if fipstate (state) eq 'CT' then position = '8'; ❸
else                position = '5';
run;
```

```
* combine selected observations from the MAPS.STATES data set
* with the observations from the Annotate data set TEMP_LABELS;

data map_labels; ❹
set maps.states temp_labels;
where fipstate (state) in ('CT','ME','MA','NH','NY','RI','VT');
run;

* use the GPROJECT procedure to project the combined data set;

proc gproject data=map_labels out=proj_map_labels; ❺
id state;
run;

* separate the combined projected data set into a map data set (MAP)
* and an Annotate data set (LABELS);

data map labels; ❻
set proj_map_labels;
if when eq 'a' then output labels; ❼
else              output map;
run;

* select a solid (MS) pattern for map areas, repeat the pattern seven times;

pattern v=ms c=graya8 r=7;

* use the GMAP procedure to create the map
* add labels using the ANNOTATE= option and the LABELS data set
* add descriptive text with a NOTE statement;

proc gmap
map=map
data=map;
id state;
choro state / discrete coutline=white nolegend annotate=labels;
note h=5 pct f='Arial/bo/it' 'MAP LABELS ON STATES MAP DATA SET';
run;
quit;
```

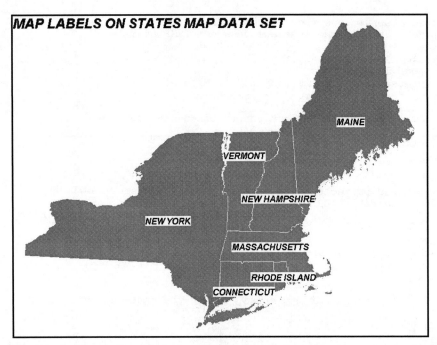

Figure 4.2   *Labels added to an originally unprojected map, now projected*

This example creates an Annotate data set. ❶ The data set is very similar to that created in Example 4.1, but the unprojected coordinates (LONG and LAT) are used as the X-Y coordinates. ❷ Note that the CONSTANT function used in this example to compute the value of pi was introduced in Version 7 of SAS and is not available in earlier versions. The unprojected coordinates are converted from degrees to radians to match the data system for unprojected X-Y coordinates in all map data sets supplied by SAS. Since the latitude for the center of Connecticut (state FIPS code 9) is approximately the same as that of Rhode Island, the label for Connecticut is placed below the X-Y coordinate location by using POSITION='8'. ❸ The Annotate data set is combined with the northeastern states map areas from the STATES map data set, ❹ and the combined data set is projected. ❺ A DATA step is used to separate the projected map data set from the projected labels. ❻ The only observations in the combined data set with a value for the variable WHEN will be from the Annotate data set. ❼ The map is drawn with PROC GMAP, with annotation added using the ANNOTATE= option. Although this process is more complicated, the map in Figure 4.2 has more detail than the map in Figure 4.1, showing the results of the extra effort.

4.3 Adding Symbols

Since symbols are only special text, the process of adding symbols to a map is much the same as that of adding text. Several fonts supplied by SAS contain symbols: MARKER, MARKERE (empty rather than filled characters from marker font), SPECIAL, and CARTOG (cartographic characters). You can display the characters in any SAS/GRAPH font using PROC GFONT.

Example 4.3 Display the SAS/GRAPH marker font

```
proc gfont name=marker nobuild showroman;  ❶
run;
quit;
```

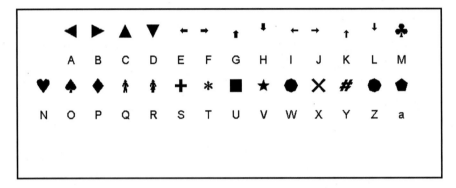

Figure 4.3 *PROC GFONT output, SAS/GRAPH marker font*

In this example, NOBUILD tells PROC GFONT that an existing font is being displayed and SHOWROMAN displays text beneath font characters.❶ The text shows characters that are used when various font characters are to be added to a map. For example, in Figure 4.3, the text shows that a "U" from the MARKER font will add a solid square, while a "V" will add a solid star. If the MARKERE font were being used, the same text would add an unfilled square or star.

Other fonts also contain special symbols and characters; for example, the SWISS font contains copyright and trademark symbols in addition to several different types of arrows. Not all font symbols are associated with characters that can be entered from a keyboard. Rather, font symbols are associated with hexadecimal codes. The hexadecimal codes can also be displayed by using the ROMHEX option:

```
proc gfont name=swiss nobuild showroman romhex;
run;
quit;
```

The 2000 census indicated that nine cities in the United States have a population in excess of one million. In order to create a map with a symbol and city name at the locations of these nine cities, you must know their longitudes and latitudes. The data set USCITY, which SAS supplies, contains information about the location of over 23,000 cities and towns in the United States. This data set has both projected (variables X and Y in radians) and unprojected (variables LONG and LAT in degrees) coordinates. The USCITY data set was used to find the projected coordinates of the nine cities.

Example 4.4 Add markers and labels, locations from USCITY data set

```
* select a font for all text and specify that all heights are expressed in
* percentages of the graphics output area;

goptions ftext='Arial/bo/it';

* create an Annotate data set from observations in the MAPS.USCITY data set
* use a WHERE statement to select only observations for nine specified
* cities output two observations for each city - one with a text label (the
* city name) the other with a symbol from the MARKER font;

data add_labels; ❶
retain
function  'label'
xsys
ysys      '2'
hsys      '3'
color     'black'
when      'a'
;
set maps.uscity (keep=state city x y); ❷
where
fipstate(state) eq 'NY' and city eq 'New York' or
fipstate(state) eq 'CA' and city in ('Los Angeles','San Diego') or
fipstate(state) eq 'IL' and city eq 'Chicago' or
fipstate(state) eq 'TX' and city in ('Houston','Dallas','San Antonio') or
fipstate(state) eq 'PA' and city eq 'Philadelphia' or
fipstate(state) eq 'AZ' and city eq 'Phoenix';

if city in ('New York','Chicago','Dallas') then position = '2'; ❸
else
if city eq 'Los Angeles' then position = '3';
else
if city in ('Philadelphia','San Antonio') then position = 'd';
else
if city eq 'San Diego' then position = 'e';
else
if city in ('Houston','Phoenix') then position = 'f';

text = city;
size = 4; cbox = 'white'; style = "'Arial/bo/it'" ; output; ❹
position = '3'; text = 'V';
size = 3; cbox = ''      ; style = "marker"          ; output; ❺

drop city state;
run;
```

```
* select a solid (MS) pattern for map areas, repeat the pattern 49 times;

pattern v=ms c=graya8 r=49;  ❻

* add descriptive text with TITLE and FOOTNOTE statements;

title     h=6        'CITIES WITH 1 MILLION+ POPULATION';
footnote  h=4  j=r 'US CENSUS BUREAU, 2000 ';

* use the GMAP procedure to create the map
* use the ANNOTATE= option and the LABELS data set to add markers and city
* names;

proc gmap map=maps.us data=maps.us;
where fipstate(state) not in ('AK','HI');
id state;
choro state / discrete coutline=white
              nolegend annotate=add_labels;  ❼
run;
quit;
```

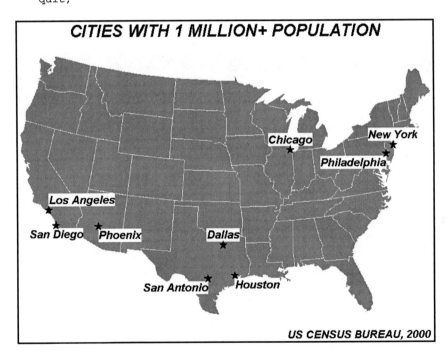

Figure 4.4 *US map data set with symbols from marker font*

This example creates the Annotate data set that will contain both symbols and text.❶ Only those variables that are constant are placed in a RETAIN statement. The USCITY data set is used to find the X-Y coordinates (projected longitude and latitude) for nine cities.❷ The POSITION used to add the city name to the map varies to prevent the text for one city from overwriting that of another.❸ The attributes of the text are set, and a white box is added as background with the CBOX option.❹ After the text is output, the font is changed to MARKER, the attributes are changed, and the box option is removed.❺ All markers are placed centered on the city location by using POSITION=5. A light-gray pattern is defined that is repeated 49 times, one for each map area to be displayed (48 states plus the District of Columbia).❻ The map is drawn with markers and labels added for all cities with a population of more than one million.❼

PROC GFONT can be used to create a font with new symbols if the appropriate symbol cannot be found in fonts supplied by SAS. User-created characters can be either new symbols used to mark locations on a map or special characters that add information about properties of map areas. An example of adding information is the gauge font. This font, which comprises a collection of 101 rectangles whose fill ranges from empty to 100% filled, is used in the next example.

More Information

The SAS code for creating the gauge font first appeared in *SAS Observations*, vol. 3, no. 1 (1993), and also appears in SAS Technical Support document TS-398. Details are shown in Appendix A4.

Example 4.5 Annotate map with the user-created gauge font

```
* select a font for all text and specify that all heights are expressed in
* percentages of the graphics output area;

goptions ftext='Arial/bo/it';

* create a format (POP) to group states by population;

proc format;
value pop
low     -<  1000000 = '<1'       1000000  -<  5000000 = '1.0-4.9'
5000000 -< 10000000 = '5.0-9.9'  10000000 -   high     = '10+'
;
run;

* create an Annotate data set (ANNO)
* extract information on location of the labels for states in specified
* areas from the MAPS.USCENTER data set - observations selected by merging
* with the US2000CO data set (Appendix A1.2), selecting WESTERN and
* MIDWESTERN states
*
* select the UNPROJECTED X-Y coordinates
* LONG and LAT and convert them from degrees to radians
*
* the text is from the GAUGE font (Appendix A4) - specific characters are
* chosen based on the percent change in population from 1990 to 2000;
```

```
data anno; ❶
retain
xsys ysys  '2'        function   'label'
style      'gauge'    when       'a'
position   '5'        color      'black'
hsys       '3'        size       5
cbox       'white'
;
merge maps.uscenter
      us2000st (where=(region in ('WEST','MIDWEST') and fipstate(state) not
                  in ('AK' 'HI')) ❷
              in=US2000);
by state;
if us2000;
x    = long * constant('pi') / 180;
y    = lat  * constant('pi') / 180; ❸
pct  = 100 * (pop2000 - pop1990) / pop1990; ❹
text = put(round(pct,1),hex2.);
run;

* combine selected observations from the MAPS.STATES data set with
* observations from the Annotate data set ANNO;

data map_anno;
set
maps.states (where=(fipstate(state) in ('AZ','CA','CO','ID','IL','IN', 'IA',
                    'KS','MI','MN','MO','MT', 'NE',
                    'NV','NM','ND','OH','OR', 'SD','UT',
                    'WA','WI','WY') and density le 2))
anno;
run;

* use the GPROJECT procedure to project the combined data set;

proc gproject data=map_anno out=projected;
id state;
run;

* separate the combined projected data set into a map data set (MAP)
* and an Annotate data set (ANNO);

data map anno; ❺
set projected;
if when eq 'a' then output anno;
else                output map;
run;

* select solid (MS) patterns for map areas, colors are shades of gray;

pattern1 v=ms c=grayfa; ❻
pattern2 v=ms c=grayda;
pattern3 v=ms c=grayaa;
pattern4 v=ms c=gray5a;

* create a LEGEND;

legend1 ❼
origin=(60,5) pct mode=share shape=bar(3,4) across=2
label=(position=top h=3 'POPULATION (MILLIONS)') value=(j=l h=3);

* add descriptive text with TITLE statements;

title1 h=6 'YEAR 2000 CENSUS POPULATION';
title2 h=4 'GAUGE SHOWS % POPULATION CHANGE, 1990 TO 2000';
```

```
* use the GMAP procedure to create the map
* add labels (symbols from the GAUGE font) using the ANNOTATE= option
* and the Annotate data set ANNO
* add descriptive text (explanation of GAUGE font levels) with a NOTE
* statement;

proc gmap
data=us2000st
map=map;
id state;
choro pop2000 / discrete coutline=black legend=legend1 annotate=anno; ❽
note j=c ❾
f=gauge h=5 '00' f='Arial/bo/it' h=3 ' = 0%    '
f=gauge h=5 '32' f='Arial/bo/it' h=3 ' = 50%   '
f=gauge h=5 '64' f='Arial/bo/it' h=3 ' = 100%  ';
format pop2000 pop.;
run;
quit;
```

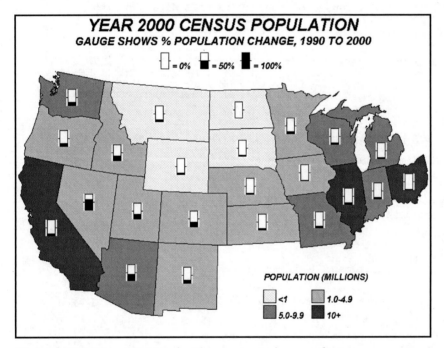

Figure 4.5 *Map annotated with user-created gauge font*

This example creates an Annotate data set with many of the same properties as in Example 4.4. ❶ The X-Y coordinate locations for the text are found by matching the population data set with the USCENTER data set. ❷ The resulting data set (ANNO) contains information only for those states in the U.S. Census Bureau WEST (excluding Alaska and Hawaii) and MIDWEST regions (see Figure 2.7). The unprojected coordinates are converted to radians and used to place the text on the map.❸ The correct character from the gauge font is chosen using the percent change in population from 1990 to 2000.❹ As was shown in Example 4.4, the Annotate data set is combined with the STATES data set, projected, then separated using a DATA step.❺ Four gray-scale patterns are defined that are used to fill map areas.❻ A LEGEND statement creates rules for the display of the map legend.❼ An ORIGIN option moves the legend to just past the midpoint (X=60 percent) and to the lower portion (Y=2) of the output area. Other legend attributes that are controlled are the shape of the bars and their orientation, ACROSS=2. The annotation and user-defined legend are added to the map.❽ A NOTE statement is used to show three values of the gauge font.❾ Since the font characters were created using hexadecimal names, the first character in the font (an empty rectangle) has a value of '01,' the midpoint '32' (50% filled), and the last character '64' (100% filled). The resulting map displays two different pieces of information for each map area. First, the gray-scale fill indicates the population group. Second, the character from the gauge font indicates how much the population has changed since 1990.

4.4 Adding Thick Borders to Map Areas

You can use the WOUTLINE= option in PROC GMAP to control the thickness of all map border lines. Values can range from 1 (the default) to 24. To create a choropleth map, the option is used with the CHORO statement, as in the following:

```
choro pop2000 / discrete coutline=black woutline=5;
```

No option can be used to change the thickness of selected border lines. In the map displayed in Figure 4.5, there is no option that can add a different style border around the WEST and MIDWEST map region to contrast with the state borders. However, Annotate data sets can add lines to maps and the thickness of the lines can be controlled.

More Information
SAS code to convert the X-Y coordinates in a map data set to an Annotate data set appeared in *SAS Observations,* vol. 5, no. 3 (1996), and modifications to that code can be found in SAS Technical Support document TS-537.

Example 4.6 Place thick borders on census regions

```
* select a font for all text and specify that all heights are expressed in
* percentages of the graphics output area;

goptions ftext='Arial/bo/it';

* create a format (POP) to group states by population;

proc format;
value pop
low       -<  1000000 = '<1'        1000000  -<  5000000 = '1.0-4.9'
5000000  -< 10000000 = '5.0-9.9'   10000000 -   high     = '10+'
;
run;
```

```
* create an Annotate data set (ANNO)
* extract information on location of the labels for states in specified
* areas from the MAPS.USCENTER data set - observations selected by merging
* with the US2000CO data set (Appendix A1.2), selecting WESTERN and
* MIDWESTERN state
*
* select the UNPROJECTED X-Y coordinates
* LONG and LAT and convert them from degrees to radians
*
* the text is from the GAUGE font (Appendix A4) - specific characters are
* chosen based on the percent change in population from 1990 to 2000;

data anno;
retain
xsys ysys  '2'        function  'label'
style      'gauge'    when      'a'
position   '5'        color     'black'
hsys       '3'        size       5
cbox       'white'
;
merge maps.uscenter
      us2000st (where=(region in ('WEST','MIDWEST') and fipstate(state) not
                in ('AK' 'HI'))
                in=US2000);
by state;
if us2000;
x    = long * constant('pi') / 180;
y    = lat  * constant('pi') / 180;
pct  = 100 * (pop2000 - pop1990) / pop1990;
text = put(round(pct,1),hex2.);
run;

* combine selected observations from the MAPS.STATES data set with
* observations from the Annotate data set ANNO;

data map_anno;
set
maps.states (where=(fipstate(state) in ('AZ','CA','CO','ID','IL','IN','IA',
                          'KS','MI','MN', 'MO','MT', 'NE', 'NV',
                          'NM', 'ND','OH','OR','SD','UT', 'WA',
                          'WI','WY') and density le 2))
anno;
run;

* use the GPROJECT procedure to project the combined data set;

proc gproject data=map_anno out=projected;
id state;
run;

* separate the combined projected data set into a map data set (MAP)
* and an Annotate data set (ANNO);

data map anno; ❶
set projected;
if when eq 'a' then output anno;
else                output map;

* add a new variable (REGION) to the projected data set MAP and
* create a new data set TWO_REGIONS;
```

```
data tworegions; ❷
set map;
if fipstate (state) in ('AZ','CA','CO','ID','MT','NV','NM','OR','UT','WA','WY')
then region = 'WEST    ';
else region = 'MIDWEST';
run;

* sort the TWO_REGIONS data set by REGION and then use the GREMOVE procedure
* to remove the internal boundaries (states) from the new map areas
* (region);

proc sort data=tworegions;
by region;
run;

proc gremove data=tworegions out=tworegions; ❸
by region;
id state;
run;

* use a data step to convert the data set TWO_REGIONS into an
* Annotate data set OUTLINE - specify thick lines using SIZE=4;

data outline; ❹
length function $8;
set tworegions;
by region segment;
retain xsys ysys '2' hsys '3' size 4 color 'black' when  'a';
if first.segment or (lag(x)=. and lag(y)=.) then function='POLY';
else                                             function='POLYCONT';
if x and y then output;
run;
* select solid (MS) patterns for map areas, colors are shades of gray;

pattern1 v=ms c=grayea; pattern2 v=ms c=grayda;
pattern3 v=ms c=grayaa; pattern4 v=ms c=gray5a;

* create a LEGEND;

legend1
origin=(60,5) pct mode=share shape=bar(3,4) across=2
label=(position=top h=3 'POPULATION (MILLIONS)') value=(j=l h=3);

* add descriptive text with TITLE statements;

title1 h=5 'YEAR 2000 CENSUS POPULATION (WEST & MIDWEST REGIONS)';
title2 h=4 'GAUGE SHOWS % POPULATION CHANGE, 1990 TO 2000';

* use the GMAP procedure to create the map
* add labels (symbols from the GAUGE font) using the ANNOTATE= option on the
* CHORO statement (use the data set ANNO)
*
* add thick borders using the ANNOTATE= option on the PROC GMAP statement
* (use the OUTLINE data set)
*
* add descriptive text (explanation of GAUGE font levels) with a NOTE
* statement;

proc gmap
data=us2000st
map=map
annotate=outline ❺
;
```

```
id state;
choro pop2000 / discrete coutline=white legend=legend1
                annotate=anno;  ❻
note j=c
f=gauge h=5 '00' f='Arial/bo/it' h=3 ' = 0%      '
f=gauge h=5 '32' f='Arial/bo/it' h=3 ' = 50%     '
f=gauge h=5 '64' f='Arial/bo/it' h=3 ' = 100%    ';
format pop2000 pop.;
run;
quit;
```

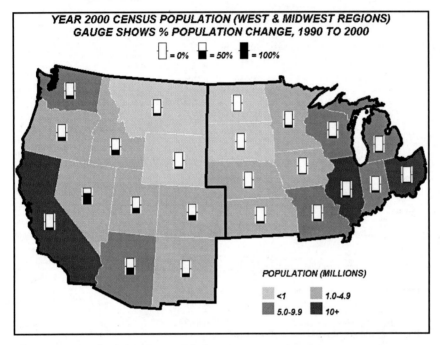

Figure 4.6 *Thick borders added to regions with an annotation*

In this example, the map data set and Annotate data set are separated from each other (following projection as a combined data set). ❶ A new data set is created from the map data set, containing a new variable that places each state in one of two census regions. ❷ PROC GREMOVE creates a new map data set with only region borders. ❸ The region boundaries data set is converted to an Annotate data set. ❹ The SIZE option controls the thickness of the lines that will be added as region borders.

You can add annotation in PROC GMAP in two ways. The thick borders are added to the map with an ANNOTATE= option in the PROC statement. ❺ Characters from the gauge font are added using an ANNOTATE= option in the CHORO statement. ❻ PROC GMAP creates a map with white borders for states, thick black borders for regions, and a gauge in the center of each state showing population change.

4.5 Adding Circles of Known Radius

The thick borders on the map in Figure 4.6 were added using annotation, specifically annotate functions that draw a polygon, POLY and POLYCONT. You can use these same functions to add a circle rather than an irregular polygon. The circle comprises many small line segments that look like a circle when joined together. The line segments are added at locations a given distance from a point (the center of the circle), with the X-Y coordinates of the ends of the lines relying on a rather complex formula that uses trigonometric functions to calculate positions on the map. The following code produces a map of the state of Texas with circles of radius 100 miles placed around three cities: Houston, Dallas, and San Antonio. The counties are shaded based on their 2000 population, using the data set TX2000CO (Appendix A1.4).

More Information

SAS code to add data-dependent circles to a map using an annotate data set appeared in *SAS Observations*, vol. 5, no. 1 (1995). The code has been modified since that publication, and the SAS code used to add circles in Example 4.7 was obtained from the revised version posted on the SAS Web site.

Example 4.7 Add circles of known radius around a given point

```
* select a font for all text and specify that all heights are expressed in
* percentages of the graphics output area;

goptions ftext='Arial/bo/it' htext=3 gunit=pct ;

* create a format (POP) to group states by population;

proc format; ❶
value pop
  low   -<    50000 = '<50'        50000  -<  100000 = '50-99'
100000 -<  500000 = '100-499'    500000  -  high     = '500+';
run;

* create an Annotate data set from observations in the MAPS.USCITY data set
* use a WHERE statement to select only observations for three cities
* the data set will contain: 1) an observation for a text label for each city
* 2) an observation for a symbol (from the MARKER font) placed on the
* location of each city, 3) 361 observations comprising a polygon
* around each city, with the polygon looking like a circle;

data anno; ❷
length function color $8 style text $15;
retain xsys ysys '2' hsys '3' color 'white' line 1 when 'a'
       radius 100 r 3949.99; ❸

set maps.uscity (keep=state city lat long);
where fipstate(state) eq 'TX' and city in ('Dallas','Houston','San
Antonio'); ❹
```

```
x=long * constant('pi') / 180; ❺
y=lat  * constant('pi') / 180;
function='label';
size=2.5; color='black'; cbox='white';
style='swissbi'; text=upcase(city); position='8'; output;
size=4;  color='white'; cbox='';

style='marker'  ; text='V' ; position='5'; output;

d2r=constant('pi') / 180;
xcen=long; ycen=lat;
size=5; style='me'; color='black';
do degree=0 to 360 by 1; ❻
   if degree=0 then function='poly';
   else             function='polycont';
   y=arsin(cos(degree*d2r)*sin(radius/R)*cos(ycen*d2r)+
           cos(radius/R)*sin(ycen*d2r))/d2r;
   x=xcen+arsin(sin(degree*d2r)*sin(radius/R)/cos(y*d2r))/d2r;
   x=x*d2r; y=y*d2r;
   output;
end;
drop state city;
run;

* combine selected observations from the MAPS.COUNTIES data set with
* observations from the Annotate data set ANNO;

data map_anno; ❼
set maps.counties (where=(fipstate(state) eq 'TX' and density le 3)) anno;
run;

* use the GPROJECT procedure to project the combined data set
* the DUPOK option is used to allow duplicate X-Y coordinates in the
* projected data set - necessary when X-Y coordinates in map boundaries are
* equal to X-Y coordinates in the Annotate data set;

proc gproject data=map_anno out=projected dupok;
id county;
run;

* separate the combined projected data set into a map data set (MAP)
* and an Annotate data set (ANNO);

data map anno;
set projected;
if when eq 'a' then output anno;
else               output map;
run;

* select solid (MS) patterns for map areas, colors are shades of gray;

pattern1 v=ms c=grayea; pattern2 v=ms c=grayba;
pattern3 v=ms c=gray8a; pattern4 v=ms c=gray5a;

* create a LEGEND;

legend1 shape=bar(3,4) origin=(5,5) pct across=2 mode=share
        label=(j=l position=top 'THOUSANDS');
```

```
* use the GMAP procedure to create the map
* use the ANNOTATE= option and data set ANNO to add the symbols, city names,
* and circles around each city;

proc gmap map=map data=tx2000co;
id county;
choro pop2000 / discrete coutline=black legend=legend1 annotate=anno;
format pop2000 pop.;

note h=4 j=r 'YEAR 2000 CENSUS POPULATION ' ❸
        j=r 'TEXAS COUNTIES '
     h=3 j=r ' '
        j=r '100 MILE RADIUS CIRCLES AROUND '
        j=r 'CITIES WITH 1 MILLION+ POPULATION ';
run;
quit;
```

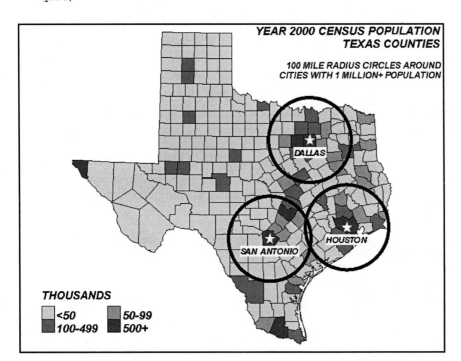

Figure 4.7 *Circles of known radius added to map with annotation*

Much of the SAS code in this example is similar to that used to create Figure 4.6. Once again, a format is created to group map areas based on their population.❶ An Annotate data set is created containing instructions to add various features to the map:❷ a marker at the location of a city; the name of the city just below the marker; a polygon with 360 small line segments, joined together to create a circle. The circles have a radius of 100 miles (radius

100), and the formula used to create the polygon uses the polar radius of the earth in miles as a constant (r=3949.99).❸ The circles are added around three cities whose locations come from the USCITY data set.❹ The location of the city is converted from degrees to radians, and instructions to include both a character from the marker font and the city's name are added to the data set.❺ A DO loop adds the instructions to create a circle.❻ The STYLE='ME' statement results in a polygon with no fill pattern, while the SIZE option controls the width of the line used to draw the circle. The RETAIN statement specifies LINE=1 for a solid line.

A rather complex formula is calculated at each pass through the loop, determining the location of the various vertices of the polygon (circle). The Annotate data set and the data set with counties from the state of Texas (from the COUNTIES map data set) are combined, projected, then separated into a projected map and Annotate data set.❼ Notice the DUPOK option used in PROC GPROJECT. The default behavior of PROC GPROJECT is to keep only unduplicated X-Y coordinates in the projected data set. In most situations, the default is adequate. However, in situations where map boundaries have been combined with an Annotate data set prior to projection, there may be duplicate X-Y coordinates in the Annotate data set alone or in combination with the map data set. This example uses a complex Annotate data set. In order to ensure that no annotate or map observations are eliminated due to duplication of X-Y location, the DUPOK option is used.

Four gray-scale patterns are defined to fill map areas, a LEGEND statement is used to create instructions for legend location and appearance, and the map is drawn with annotation using PROC GMAP.❽ Using a NOTE in lieu of a TITLE leaves more room for the map (as did specifying MODE=SHARE in the LEGEND statement).

More Information
To learn more about using Annotate to enhance your maps, see *Annotate: Simply the Basics* by Art Carpenter (1999).

CHAPTER 5

Creating Maps for Various Output Destinations

5.1   Chapter Overview

When you run any SAS/GRAPH procedure in display manager mode, the default destination of output is the GRAPH window (that is, your monitor). Though you can print the contents of this window, you can produce higher-quality hardcopy output by specifying a device driver other than the default in a GOPTIONS statement. You can also produce output to be included in word processing documents or posted on a Web page. Producing such output requires an understanding of output devices and graphics stream files. This chapter explains how to direct SAS/GRAPH output to hardcopy output devices and to graphics stream files.

5.2   Hardcopy Output

You can direct SAS/GRAPH output to a printer or plotter using a GOPTIONS statement and a DEVICE= (or DEV=) option that specifies the device on which the output will be produced. If you are using SAS/GRAPH in a Windows environment and have selected a PostScript printer as your default Windows printer, the following statement would direct your SAS/GRAPH output to that printer:

```
goptions device=ps;
```

If your default Windows printer is a PCL printer that supports PCL Level 5, you could use

```
goptions device=pcl5;
```

The GDEVICE procedure will create a list of device drivers supported by SAS/GRAPH.

```
proc gdevice c=sashelp.devices nofs;
    list _all_;
    run;
quit;
```

When you are in display manager mode, this code produces a list of device drivers in the output window. Each supported device driver is associated with a number of device-specific attributes, such as fonts and colors. The GDEVICE procedure can also be used to list the attributes of any given device.

```
proc gdevice c=sashelp.devices nofs;
    list ps;
    run;
quit;
```

Fonts and colors are discussed more fully in Chapter 2. You can use fonts supplied by SAS with any device. There are also hardware fonts that are available only with specific devices; for example, Helvetica is available only on PostScript printers or when you are creating graphics output as PostScript or PDF files. TrueType fonts can be used with some device drivers in the

Windows environment. Although color is an attribute of all portions of graphics output (text, fill patterns for map areas, lines that outline map areas, features added with annotation), the ability to produce color output is device specific.

5.3 Graphics Stream Files

The term graphics stream file (GSF) refers to an external file produced by SAS/GRAPH that contains graphics commands. The external file can be used in three ways: it can be sent to a printer using host operating system commands, incorporated into a word processing document, or posted for viewing on a Web page. Creating a graphics stream file requires GOPTIONS and FILENAME statements. The syntax is

```
filename <filcref> "<external file name>";
goptions device=<devicename> gsfname=<fileref>;
```

A number of device drivers supported by SAS/GRAPH can only be used to produce external files and must be used in combination with a FILENAME statement. These include GIF, JPEG, EPS (Encapsulated PostScript), CGM, and PDF. All of the SAS/GRAPH output in this book was produced using the GIF device driver—for example, using these statements:

```
filename gout "i:\example1.gif"
goptions device=gif gsfname=gout;
```

The GIF files were inserted into a word processing document.

5.4 Maps for Web Posting

There are a number of different ways to create maps for posting on the Web. The choice of a device driver to use in creating such output is dictated by how the map is to be used once it is made available on a Web page. If you want a static map (one that will just be viewed and possibly printed), either the GIF or PDF format is a good choice. You can create a map with hyperlinked map areas (referred to as a map with drill-down capabilities) using the Output Delivery System (ODS) in conjunction with the GIF device driver. The JAVA, JAVAMETA, and ACTIVEX device drivers enable the creation of maps with pop-up information. The animated GIF and JAVAMETA device drivers allow you to add another dimension to map information, in that a series of maps can be viewed showing the change in the spatial distribution of a response variable over time. Though these formats represent a wide array of choices, they are only a sampling of Web-enabled mapping possibilities.

5.4.1 Static Maps (GIF versus ODS+PDF)

Static maps are those whose only purpose is display and/or printing. Two common formats for creating static maps are GIF and PDF. Both GIF and PDF files have advantages and disadvantages. GIF-based maps are readily displayed in any Internet browser. They can also be used in other applications, such as pasted into a word processing document. However, since they are bit-mapped, how they will look on a user's monitor depends on a number of factors that cannot be controlled during map creation or posting. For example, a map produced with the following options will be too large for the entire map to appear within the screen display of a browser on a low-resolution monitor.

```
filename gout 'i:\example1.gif';
goptions device=gif gsfname=gout xpixels=800 ypixels=600;
```

On a high-resolution monitor, the map might look very small. In addition to the map, any text displayed will vary in height as a function of monitor resolution and user-specific browser setup.

Maps created using the PDF format require a browser plug-in (Adobe Acrobat), but maps can be fit into a page without concern for variation in browser setup or monitor configuration.

```
ods listing close;
ods pdf file="i:\testmaps.pdf";
<proc gmap statements>
ods pdf close;
ods listing
```

If multiple maps are written to the file TESTMAPS.PDF, they will be visible on multiple pages within the PDF file.

5.4.2 Drill-Down Maps (ODS+GIF)

Map areas can be linked to additional information by using a combination of ODS and the GIF device driver. In addition to drill-down from map areas, the map legend can also be linked to other Web pages. The map in the next example has hyperlinks to both state and regional data. Two assumptions are made: both the HTML file (CENSUS2000.HTM) and the GIF file (REGIONS.GIF) will be created in a local environment (written to directory C:\) and then moved to the same location (directory) on a Web server; the HTML files linked to map areas (states) and legend boxes are created independent of this example and placed in the same location on the Web server as the HTML and GIF files.

Example 5.1A Create a map with drill-down capabilities

```
* add two variables to the population data set
* new variables are used to link map areas (states) and legend boxes
* (regions) to previously created HTML files;

data links; ❶
set us2000st;
state_link = 'ALT="' || trim(fipname(state)) || '" href=state'
                     || put(state,z2.) || '.htm'; ❷
select(region);
   when ('NORTHEAST') region_link = 'ALT="NORTHEAST" href=northeast.htm'; ❸
   when ('SOUTH')     region_link = 'ALT="SOUTH"     href=south.htm';
   when ('MIDWEST')   region_link = 'ALT="MIDWEST"   href=midwest.htm';
   when ('WEST')      region_link = 'ALT="WEST"      href=west.htm';
end;
run;

goptions device=gif xpixels=1000 ypixels=750 ftext='Arial' gunit=pct; ❹

ods listing close;
ods html path='c:\' (url=none) file="census2000.htm"; ❺

pattern1 v=ms c=grayca; pattern2 v=ms c=gray9a;
pattern3 v=ms c=gray6a; pattern4 v=ms c=gray3a;

legend1 shape=bar(3,4) origin=(88,15) pct mode=share ❻
        label=none value=(font='Arial/bo/it' h=2) across=1;

title    h=8 'US CENSUS BUREAU REGIONS';
footnote h=3
   'CLICK ON STATE OR LEGEND BOX TO DRILL DOWN TO YEAR 2000 CENSUS DATA';

* data set links used as the response data set
* it contains variables used to link map areas (STATE_LINK) and the
* legend (REGION_LINK) to previously created HTML files;

proc gmap map=maps.us data=links;
id state;
choro region / midpoints='NORTHEAST' 'SOUTH' 'MIDWEST' 'WEST'
               html=state_link ❼
               html_legend=region_link ❽
               coutline=white legend=legend1 name='regions';❾
run;
quit;

ods html close; ❿
ods listing;
```

The data set US2000ST (see Appendix A1.1 for a description) contains a FIPS number and region name for each of the 50 states and the District of Columbia. A new data set is created from that data set, adding two variables that link states (map areas) and regions (legend boxes) to additional information in the form of HTML files.❶ The value of the variable STATE_LINK link comprises an ALT tag (ALT=), a hyperlink (HREF=), and a filename that is the link destination.❷ For example, South Dakota is state number 46. The value of variable STATE_LINK is

```
ALT="SOUTH DAKOTA" href=state46.htm
```

If you place the mouse pointer over South Dakota, the ALT tag will cause the state name to appear as shown in Figure 5.1. When you press the left mouse button, a link is made to the file STATE46.HTM. Similar values are given to the variable REGION_LINK that will be used to link the legend.❸ South Dakota is in the Midwest, so the value of the variable REGION_LINK is

```
ALT="MIDWEST" href=midwest.htm
```

A GOPTIONS statement sets a size for the map in pixels and chooses a font and units for height of all text.❹ An ODS statement is used to request HTML output, written to a file named CENSUS2000.HTM in the directory C:\ specified with the PATH option.❺ The HTML file will contain a reference to a GIF file created with the GMAP procedure. The option (URL=NONE) requests that no information from the PATH option be used to build the hyperlink for the IMG tag that ODS will create within the file CENSUS2000.HTM. This requires that both the HTML and GIF files be in the same location (directory) when posted on a Web server.

A LEGEND statement controls the placement and appearance of the legend.❻ The data set LINKS is used as the response data set. The variable STATE_LINK is used as the HTML variable, linking map areas to state-specific HTML files.❼ The variable REGION_LINK is used as the HTML_LEGEND variable, linking the legend boxes to region-specific HTML files.❽ The NAME= option is used to name the GIF file produced with the GMAP procedure.❾ This name (REGIONS.GIF) appears in the HTML file CENSUS2000.HTM. Once the procedure is complete, the ODS destination is closed.❿

The SAS code in Example 5.1A produces two files. The first is a file of HTML commands that was named in the ODS HTML statement. That file contains all the links to other files (the HREF statements) and definitions of polygons (AREA SHAPE="POLY" statements) that define the areas on the screen that are linked to files. The second file is named using an option in the CHORO statement in PROC GMAP, NAME='REGIONS'. This is a GIF file that is referenced in the HTML file.

```
<IMG SRC="regions.gif" border="0" USEMAP="#idx_map">
```

The map areas in the GIF file have a one-to-one correspondence to the polygons defined in the HTML file. The links are in the file CENSUS2000.HTM, while the image displayed on the screen is contained in REGIONS.GIF. If the NAME= option is left out of PROC GMAP, the procedure assigns default names: GMAP.GIF, GMAP1.GIF, etc.

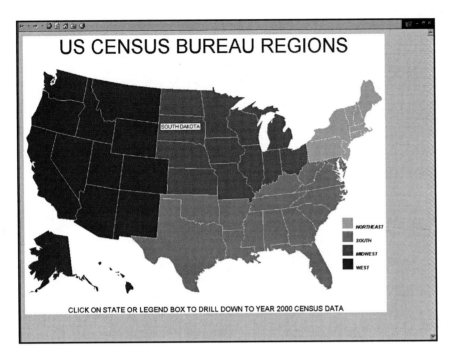

Figure 5.1 *Map with drill-down areas and a legend*

Rather than create hyperlinked map areas and/or legend boxes, you can add hyperlinks to symbols that have been placed on a map with annotation. The next map contains symbols (stars) and text (city names), with the stars linked to other data in much the same way that map areas were linked in the last example.

Example 5.1B Drill-down city markers added with Annotate

```
* create an Annotate data set containing a variable (HTML) that links
* part of the annotation (STARS) to previously created HTML files;

data add_labels; ❶
retain
xsys
ysys        '2'
hsys        '3'
color       'black'
when        'a'
;
input text $12. x y position : $1.;
size = 4; cbox = 'white'; style = "'Arial/bo/it'" ; output;
html='HREF="' || trim(compress(text)) || '.htm"'; ❷
size = 3; cbox = ''; style = "marker"; position = '5'; text = 'V'; output;
```

```
datalines; ❸
New York      0.28540  0.09317 2
Los Angeles  -0.32135 -0.01648 3
Chicago       0.10520  0.08526 2
Houston       0.00664 -0.13007 f
Philadelphia  0.27260  0.07840 d
Phoenix      -0.23387 -0.04455 f
San Diego    -0.30851 -0.04273 e
Dallas       -0.01374 -0.07733 2
San Antonio  -0.04075 -0.13493 d
;
run;

pattern v=ms c=graya8 r=49;

goptions device=gif ftext='Arial/bo/it'; ❹

ods listing close;
ods html path='c:\' (url=none) file='cities.htm';

title1  h=6 pct 'CITIES WITH 1 MILLION+ POPULATION';
title2  h=4 pct 'CLICK ON A STAR TO ACCESS CITY-SPECIFIC DATA';

footnote h=4 pct j=r 'US CENSUS BUREAU, 2000 ';

* use the Annotate data set to add text (CITY NAMES), symbols (STARS),
* and hyperlinks to the map;

proc gmap map=maps.us data=maps.us;
where state not in (2 15);
id state;
choro state / discrete coutline=white nolegend
              annotate=add_labels ❺
              name='cities'; ❻
run;
quit;

ods html close;
ods listing;
```

An Annotate data set is created.❶ The data set contains a variable named HTML.❷ The value of the variable HTML is a hyperlink. Note that the name of the variable in an Annotate data set that contains a hyperlink must be HTML. In this example, it links the text (a star from the marker font) to a specified file. The linked file has the same name as the city just read from the DATALINES file (with embedded spaces removed using the COMPRESS function). The city names, their locations, and the position to be used for adding the city name to the map are located in a DATALINES file.❸

An ODS statement gives a name (CITIES.HTM) to the HTML file to be created by the GMAP procedure.❹ The URL=NONE option requests that no path be added to the name of the GIF file that will be embedded in the HTML file. The Annotate data set is used in the GMAP procedure to add symbols and stars to the map.❺ The HTML variable in the Annotate data set links the stars to HTML files. A NAME= option names the GIF file (CITIES) produced by the GMAP procedure.❻

The HTML and GIF files produced by the GMAP procedure are created in a local environment and placed in directory C:\ as a result of the PATH= option in the ODS statement. Both the HTML file (CITIES.HTM) and the GIF file (CITIES.GIF) must be placed in the same location on a Web server. No path is specified on any of the hyperlinks created by the Annotate data set. Thus, all the linked HTML files must also be placed in the same location on the Web server as the HTML and GIF files. It is assumed that the linked HTML files with information about the various cities were previously created.

5.4.3 Maps with "Pop-up" Information (ODS+JAVA)

Rather than linking map areas to files that contain additional data, you can create maps with information that pops up when the mouse pointer passes over a map area. Pop-up boxes are the least complex of the many features of the JAVA device driver. The information in the pop-up box is controlled by the ID and response variables used in PROC GMAP. The GIF files produced in Examples 5.1A and 5.1B are "stand-alone," meaning they can be displayed just by using a Web browser. The file produced by the JAVA device driver is not stand-alone, so it requires a Java applet (MAPAPP.JAR) to display properly.

Example 5.2 Pop-up information (JAVA device driver)

```
goptions device=java xpixels=1000 ypixels=750
        ftext='Arial' htext=3 ctext=black gunit=pct; ❶

* use the ATTRIBUTES= option to specify the location of the MAPAPP.JAR
* applet on the Web server
* output (HTML file) created locally, to be moved to the Web server later;

ods listing close;
ods html file="c:\usa2000.htm"
        codebase="http://webservername/graph/"; ❷

* add a new variable (STATE_NAME) to both the map and response data sets
* the variable will be used as the ID variable in PROC GMAP;

data usa;
set maps.us;
state_name = fipname(state); ❸
run;

* add a label and format to the response variable in the response data set
* these attributes control appearance of the pop-up information;

data pop;
set us2000st;
state_name = fipname(state); ❹
label state_name = 'State Name'
      pop2000 = 'Year 2000 Census Population';
format pop2000 comma15.;
run;
```

```
pattern1 v=ms c=gray88 r=51;  ❺

title1 j=l h=6 'YEAR 2000 CENSUS POPULATION';
title2 j=l h=4 '(PLACE MOUSE POINTER OVER STATE TO SHOW POPULATION)';

proc gmap map=usa data=pop;  ❻
id state_name;
choro pop2000 / coutline=white nolegend;
run;
quit;

ods html close;  ❼
ods listing;
```

In this example, the JAVA device driver is selected, the size of the image is defined in pixels, and text attributes are selected.❶ The Output Delivery System (ODS) is used to produce a file (C:\USA2000.HTM) that will contain a mixture of HTML commands and JavaScript.❷ The CODEBASE= option is used to specify the location of the Java applet MAPAPP.JAR that is required to display map output produced by the JAVA device driver. The text will be embedded in the HTML file created by the GMAP procedure, and should point to a location that is accessible by users who will access the file USA2000.HTM once it is moved to a Web server.

The US2000ST data set contains a state FIPS code, not a state name. The value of the ID variable in PROC GMAP is displayed in the hover text. Therefore, a new variable is added to the data set, STATE_NAME, which will be used as the ID variable in PROC GMAP.❸ A format and label are added to the variable POP2000, the response variable used later in creating the map.❹ The response variable is also displayed in the hover text, and the COMMA format facilitates reading the population. If labels are associated with variables, they will be displayed in place of variable names. POP2000 already has a label in the data set US2000ST—"Year 2000 Census Population." A label is added to STATE_NAME. The PATTERN statement is repeated 51 times, one for each state plus the District of Columbia.❺ PROC GMAP creates the map,❻ and the ODS destination is closed.❼

Example 5.2 produces only one file, USA2000.HTM. It is created in the local environment (in the directory C:\) and contains both the area definitions and the map display. This differs from the previous two examples in which two files were created, one containing an HTML file and one containing a GIF file. The pop-up box shown in Figure 5.2 shows the values of the ID and response variables from PROC GMAP. The labels for both variables are displayed, and the response variable is formatted. There are many other options of varying complexity associated with the JAVA device. One of them is the same type of drill-down feature created in Examples 5.1A and 5.1B. This simple example displays just one useful feature that is very easy to implement.

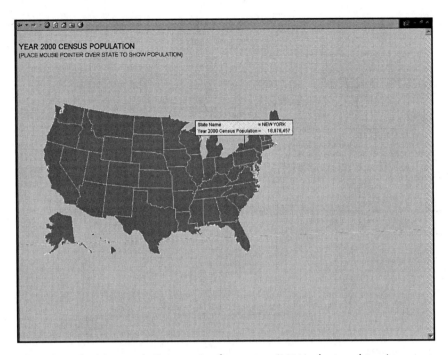

Figure 5.2 *Map with "pop-up" information (JAVA device driver)*

5.4.4 *Maps with "Pop-up" Information (JAVAMETA)*

The pop-up information available with the JAVA device driver is limited to values associated with the ID and response variables in the response data set. The JAVAMETA device driver allows you to create TIPS—user-defined information that will appear in the pop-up box associated with any given map area. Just as output produced with the JAVA device driver requires access to a JAVA applet, output produced with the JAVAMETA device driver requires access to the MetaViewApplet (METAFILE.ZIP) to display properly.

The following SAS code produces a map with pop-up boxes that show the state name, the population in both 1990 and 2000, and the percentage change in population from 1990 to 2000.

Example 5.3 Pop-up information (JAVAMETA device driver)

```
proc format;
value pop
low      -< 1300000 = '<1.3'
1300000 -< 4000000 = '1.3-3.9'
4000000 -< 6000000 = '4.0-5.9'
6000000 -  high     = '6.0+'
;
run;
```

```
* text to put in floating text box (after line with TIP);

data popup; ❶
length popvar $200;
set us2000st;
pct    = 100*(pop2000 - pop1990) / pop1990;
stname = fipname(state);
popvar = 'tip=['||
         quote(stname) || ' ' ||
         quote('POPULATION')   || ' ' ||
         quote('1990 :  '  ||  put(pop1990,comma10.)) || ' ' ||
         quote('2000 :  '  ||  put(pop2000,comma10.)) || ' ' ||
         quote('% CHANGE :  ' || put(pct,10.1))
         || ']'; ❷
run;

* reserved filename for javameta device driver;
filename _webout 'c:\jm.htm'; ❸

* write HTML header with selected options;

data _null_; ❹
file _webout;
input;
put _infile_;
datalines;
<html>
<head>
<title>JAVAMETA DEVICE DRIVER</title>
</head>
<body>
<applet archive="http://webservername/graph/metafile.zip" ❺
        code="MetaViewApplet.class"
        width="800" height="600" align="TOP">

<param name="BackgroundColor"    value="0xFFFFFF"> ❻
<param name="DataTipStyle"       value="Stick_Fixed">
<param name="ZoomControlEnabled" value="False">
<param name="Metacodes"          value="
;
run;

goptions device=javameta ❼
         gunit=pct
         ftext='HelveticaBold'
         htext=3.75
         htitle=7.25;

pattern1 v=ms c=grayfa;
pattern2 v=ms c=grayca;
pattern3 v=ms c=grayaa;
pattern4 v=ms c=gray5a;

legend1
label=(j=r 'MILLIONS')
shape=bar(3,4)
across=4
;
```

```
title 'YEAR 2000 CENSUS POPULATION';

* add metagraphics from PROC GMAP;

proc gmap ❽
map=maps.us
data=popup
imagemap=temp;
id state;
choro  pop2000 / discrete coutline=black legend=legend1 html=popvar;
format pop2000 pop.;
run;
quit;

* write HTML footer;

data _null_; ❾
file _webout mod;
input;
put _infile_;
datalines;
">
    SORRY, YOUR BROWSER DOES NOT SUPPORT THIS APPLICATION
</applet>
</body>
</html>
;
run;

filename _webout; ❿
```

In this example, the response data set US2000ST is used to create a new data set, POPUP.❶ The percentage change in population from 1990 to 2000 is calculated and placed in variable PCT. Another variable, POPVAR, is created that contains the contents of the pop-up box that will appear when the mouse pointer is placed over a map area (a state).❷ The text "TIP=[" is followed by a series of quoted text strings that will show the following: line 1, the state name; line 2, the text "POPULATION"; line 3, the text "1990:" followed by the value of the variable POP1990; line 4, the text "2000:" followed by the value of the variable POP2000; line 5, the text "% CHANGE" followed by the value of the variable PCT. Variables POP1990 and POP2000 are formatted to display with commas.

A FILENAME statement is used to associate the fileref _WEBOUT with an external file (C:\JM.HTM).❸ _WEBOUT is recognized by the JAVAMETA device driver and is opened in APPEND mode when a SAS/GRAPH procedure directs output to the external file assigned to _WEBOUT. Since the JAVAMETA device driver produces only metacodes, a DATA step is used to add an HTML header to the file.❹ The location of the applet (METAFILE.ZIP), needed to display the metacodes as a graphics image, is specified.❺ This location must be accessible to users of your Web site. Various parameters that control the options available with the JAVAMETA device driver are written to the HTML file.❻

A number of options are available, and these parameters only refer to a small subset: a background color is specified; the DataTipStyle parameter controls the style of the tip when the cursor is placed over a map area (Stick_Fixed connects a line from the center of the area to the pop-up box); ZoomControlEnabled is assigned a value of FALSE, disabling the default placement of a zoom control at the bottom of the graphics output; the text METACODES=" is placed in the HTML file and will be followed by the metacodes produced by the JAVAMETA device driver and the GMAP procedure.

A GOPTIONS statement specifies the JAVAMETA device driver and two options: a font for all text (Helvetica Bold), and the height for TITLE1 (HTITLE) and all other text (HTEXT) expressed in terms of percentage of the output area (GUNIT=PCT).❼ The response data set is POPUP. The HTML= option specifies the variable (POPVAR) in the response data set that contains the information to be displayed in the pop-up window.❽ The IMAGEMAP= option is needed in combination with the HTML= option to add the pop-up box TIP values to the map. Another DATA step is used to write a footer to the HTML file.❾ This text will be added after the metacodes. Notice that the MOD option must be used in the FILE statement to add this additional text. A FILENAME statement deassigns the _WEBOUT fileref.❿

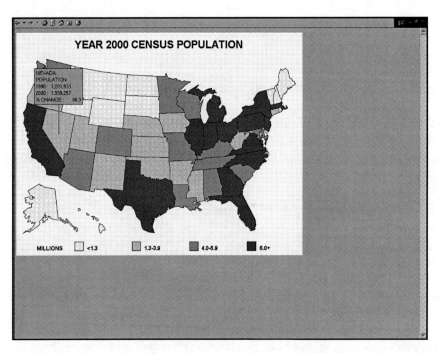

Figure 5.3 *Map with "enhanced pop-up" information (JAVAMETA device driver)*

The pop-up box in Figure 5.3 shows the TIP created in the first DATA step of Example 5.3. The additional information shows the population of Nevada in both 1990 and 2000, plus the fact that Nevada experienced a 66% increase in population over that 10-year period. Many other options available with the JAVAMETA device driver are not addressed by this example. Also, starting with Release 8.1 of SAS/GRAPH, ODS can be used together with the JAVAMETA device driver to create the HTML file in which the metacodes are contained. Without ODS, you have more control of the use of various JAVAMETA device driver features.

5.4.5 Maps with "Pop-up" Information (ODS+ACTIVEX)

The ACTIVEX device driver also can create a map with information that pops up as the mouse pointer passes over map areas. As with the JAVA device driver, the pop-up capability is only one of many features that are available in a map created with the ACTIVEX device driver. The following example creates a prism map using ODS and the ACTIVEX device driver.

Example 5.4 Pop-up information (ACTIVEX device driver)

```
* add a new variable (STATE_NAME) to both the map and response data sets
* the variable will be used as the ID variable in PROC GMAP;

data usa;
set maps.us;
state_name = fipname(state); ❶
run;

* add a label and format to the response variable in the response data set
* these attributes control the appearance of the pop-up information;

data pop;
set us2000st;
state_name = fipname(state); ❷
label state_name = 'STATE'
      pop2000 = 'POPULATION';
format pop2000 comma15.;
run;

ods listing close;
ods html file="c:\ax_prism.htm"
attributes=(codebase="http://webservername/graph/sasgraph.exe"); ❸

goptions device   = activex ❹
         xpixels  = 800
         ypixels  = 600
         cback    = white
         gunit    = pct
         ftext    = 'Helvetica'
         htitle   = 7
         htext    = 4
         border;

pattern1 v=ms c=grayfa;
pattern2 v=ms c=grayca;
pattern3 v=ms c=gray9a;
pattern4 v=ms c=gray5a;
```

```
legend1
label=('QUARTILE')
value=(j=1 'FIRST' 'SECOND' 'THIRD' 'FOURTH')  ❺
;

title 'YEAR 2000 CENSUS POPULATION';
proc gmap
map=usa
data=pop
;
id state_name;
prism  pop2000 / levels=4 legend=legend1 coutline=black;  ❻
run;
quit;

ods html close;
ods listing;
```

As with the JAVA device driver, the value of the ID variable used in the GMAP procedure appears in the pop-up box. A new variable (STATE_NAME) is added to the map data set (USA) to be used later as the ID variable in PROC GMAP.❶ The variable STATE_NAME is also added to the response data set (POP).❷ Again, as with the JAVA device driver, the value of the response variable (POP2000) also appears in the pop-up box together with the variable label. A format and a label are added as attributes of the response variable to control its appearance in the pop-up box.

External files created with the JAVA and JAVAMETA device drivers require access to applets in order to display when accessed on a Web server; the applets are MAPAPP.JAR and METAFILE.ZIP, respectively. An ACTIVEX file also requires access to an application. The applets required to view JAVA- and JAVAMETA-produced files can reside on the Web server. The application used to display graphics produced with the ACTIVEX device driver must reside locally. For example, if you are attempting to view ACTIVEX-produced maps on a PC that is being used to browse Web pages, the application must reside on that PC. An ODS HTML statement with an ATTRIBUTES= option is used to point to the location on a Web server of an application supplied by SAS (SASGRAPH.EXE).❸ If the software needed to display the ACTIVEX graphics is not found on the PC requesting display of the ACTIVEX graphics, a user will be offered the opportunity to download and install the required software. The ODS statement is also used to direct the output of the GMAP procedure to a file (AX_PRISM.HTM) in the local environment (in the directory C:\). This file can later be moved to a location on a Web server.

The ACTIVEX device driver is selected together with a number of device options.❹ A LEGEND statement creates a legend to be used with the GMAP procedure.❺ Several options are used with the PRISM statement in PROC GMAP.❻ Rather than using the DISCRETE option and a FORMAT statement for the response variable as was done in Example 1.2, the LEVELS option groups the map areas (states) into quartiles (LEVELS=4) based on the value of the response variable (POP2000). States are outlined in black and the LEGEND statement is used to label the LEGEND boxes as quartiles.

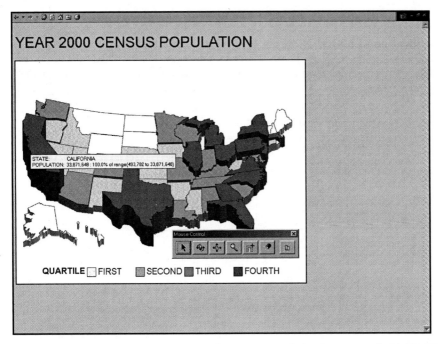

Figure 5.4 *Map with "pop-up" information and display controls (ACTIVEX device driver)*

The map is displayed in Figure 5.4. In addition to the values of the ID and response variables, the pop-up box also displays the value of the response variable for the selected map area as a percentage of the maximum value of the response variable in the response data set. California is the state with the largest population, so 100% is displayed. Also shown in Figure 5.4 is one of the control box menus available by clicking the right mouse button anytime the mouse pointer is within the box surrounding the map. The "Mouse Control" menu is displayed and can be used to change the function of the mouse pointer. For example, selecting the magnifying glass allows you to zoom in on map areas.

Notice that the states grouped in the various quartiles differ in height within quartiles. In Figure 1.2 (also a prism map), all states within a given group had the same height. The prism map created using the ACTIVEX device driver shows the difference between the values of the response variable with map area groups.

5.5 Multiple Maps (JAVAMETA)

The JAVAMETA device driver can be used to create a series of maps that show counties with varying percentages of population change over time. You can select any map in the series using a drop-down menu located at the bottom center of the Web page display. The SAS code in Example 5.5 is used to create four maps.

Example 5.5 Multiple maps—varying levels population change

```
%macro popchange(diff,change,outfile); ❶

   data countyok (keep=fmtname start label);
   retain fmtname '$county' label 'OK';
   set us2000co;
   if (pop2000 - pop1990) / pop1990 &diff; ❷
   start = put(state,z2.) || put(county,z3.);
   run;

   proc format cntlin=countyok;
   run;

   data counties;
   set maps.counties;
   stcou = put(state,z2.) || put(county,z3.);
   if put(stcou,$county.) eq 'OK';
   drop stcou;
   run;

   data state_county;
   set maps.states   (in=from_states)
       counties;
   where fipstate(state) not in ('AK', 'HI', 'PR') and density le 3;
   if from_states then dummy=1;
   else                dummy=2;
   run;

   proc gproject
   data=state_county
   out=projected_counties
   ;
   id state county;
   run;

   filename _webout "&outfile"; ❸

   goptions device=javameta ❹
            gunit=pct
            ftext='HelveticaItalicBold'
            htext=4.00
            htitle=4.75;

   pattern1 v=me c=black;
   pattern2 v=ms c=grayc8;

   title1  "COUNTIES WITH A &change IN POPULATION"; ❺
   title2  "1990 TO 2000";

   footnote j=l 'US CENSUS BUREAU';
```

```
      proc gmap ❻
      map=projected_counties
      data=projected_counties
      all;
      id state county;
      choro dummy / discrete coutline=black nolegend;
      run;
      quit;

      filename _webout; ❼

   %mend;

   %popchange(le -.05,  5+% DECREASE, c:\popchng1.txt); ❽
   %popchange(ge  .10, 10+% INCREASE, c:\popchng2.txt);
   %popchange(ge  .25, 25+% INCREASE, c:\popchng3.txt);
   %popchange(ge  .50, 50+% INCREASE, c:\popchng4.txt);
```

The same SAS code will be used multiple times, varying three items to create maps with different content. The macro has three arguments.❶ The first argument, DIFF, specifies the change in population used to select counties for display. The second argument, CHANGE, is used in the map title. The last argument, OUTFILE, specifies the name of the file created by the GMAP procedure. The macro variable &DIFF is used in the DATA step that selects counties for display,❷ while the macro variable &OUTFILE is used in a FILENAME statement.❸ All output is created in the local environment, in the directory C:\. The JAVAMETA device driver is specified.❹

The macro variable &CHANGE is used in a TITLE statement.❺ The GMAP procedure creates a map.❻ After map creation, the fileref _WEBOUT is deassigned.❼ The macro is used to create four maps.❽

An HTML file is needed to display the four maps.

```
   <html> ❶
   <head>
   <title>JAVAMETA DEVICE DRIVER</title>
   </head>
   <body>

   <applet archive="http://webservername/graph/metafile.zip"
     code="MetaViewApplet.class"
     width="800" height="600" align="TOP"> ❷

     <param name="BackgroundColor"        value="0xffffff"> ❸
     <param name="ZoomControlEnabled"     value="False">
     <param name="SlideShowControlEnabled" value="False">

     <param name="Metacodes"  value="http://webservername/graph/popchng4.txt"> ❹
     <param name="Metacodes1" value="http://webservername/graph/popchng3.txt">
     <param name="Metacodes2" value="http://webservername/graph/popchng2.txt">
     <param name="Metacodes3" value="http://webservername/graph/popchng1.txt">

     <param name="MetacodesLabel"  value="  50+% POPULATION INCREASE  "> ❺
     <param name="Metacodes1Label" value="  25+% POPULATION INCREASE  ">
     <param name="Metacodes2Label" value="  10+% POPULATION INCREASE  ">
     <param name="Metacodes3Label" value="   5+% POPULATION DECREASE  ">
```

```
     SORRY, YOUR BROWSER DOES NOT SUPPORT THIS APPLICATION ❻
</applet>

</body> ❼
</html>
```

Minimal HTML code is used in the first ❶ and last ❼ portions of the file. This code surrounds statements that are specific to the display of the metacodes produced by the JAVAMETA device driver. The code beginning with <APPLET specifies the location of the application METAFILE.ZIP on the Web server.❷ The size (800 x 600) and position of the display are also specified. The application recognizes a number of different parameters. The first set ❸ selects a background color (WHITE) and turns off two of the default display controls (the ZOOM and SLIDE SHOW controls). The next set gives the name and location on the Web server of the four files that were created with the SAS code in Example 5.5 and then moved to a Web server.❹ The final set of parameters creates the text that will appear in a drop-down menu box that allows selection of any of the four maps.❺ If the browser is unable to display the map, the message beginning with "SORRY" will be displayed in place of the maps.❻

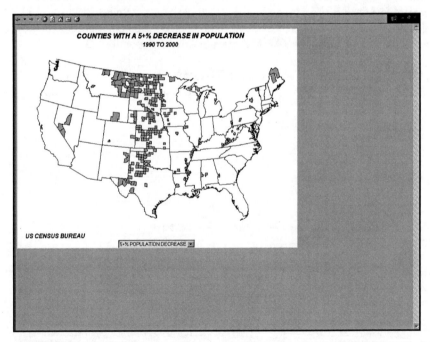

Figure 5.5 *Map with drop-down menu for map selection (JAVAMETA device driver)*

The fourth map (metacodes in the file POPCHNG1.TXT) is shown in Figure 5.5. A user of the Web page can choose what map to view, using the drop-down menu box displayed below the map.

5.5.1   Animation (JAVAMETA and GIFANIM)

The maps in Figures 4.5 and 4.6 have a time dimension. In addition to showing the spatial distribution of population in the year 2000, these maps have symbols from the gauge font that allow the display of a measure of population change between 1990 and 2000. The pop-up box in Figure 5.3 also add a time dimension by showing both 1990 and 2000 populations plus the percentage change over the 10-year period.

Another approach to adding a time dimension is to use animation. A series of maps is displayed showing changes in the spatial distribution of the response variable from map to map. Animated maps can be created with PROC GMAP in two ways—using either the JAVAMETA or the GIFANIM device driver. The JAVAMETA device driver allows creation of a slide show, using an applet to display a number of individual files with a preset time delay. The GIFANIM device driver creates one stand-alone file (which does not require another application for viewing) that contains all the maps to be displayed.

The same task is repeated to show how to use both device drivers. The location of the geographic center of the population of the United States is to be mapped over the period 1790 through 2000. A map will be displayed at every 10-year interval, showing how the location of the center moves west and slightly south over time. The center during any given year will be marked by a star, while that of previous years will be shown with a triangle. The first title on each map will contain text showing the year currently displayed, while the second will show the county and state of the population center during that year. The state in which the center is located will be filled with gray.

Example 5.6 Map animation—JAVAMETA device driver

```
* create an Annotate data set - used to place a symbol at the location of
* the US population center in each of the years in the DATALINES file;

data popctr; ❶
    retain function 'label' xsys ysys '2' hsys '3' position '5' ❷
           size 3.5 color 'black' style 'marker' text 'C' when 'a';

    infile datalines dsd;
    input year : $4. y x location : $40.;

    fips = stfips(scan(location,-1)); ❸
    y    = y*constant('pi')/180;
    x    = x*constant('pi')/180;

    datalines;
    1790,  39.275,  76.187,  "KENT COUNTY,MD"
    1800,  39.268,  76.943,  "HOWARD COUNTY,MD"
    1810,  39.192,  77.620,  "LOUDON COUNTY,VA"
    1820,  39.095,  78.550,  "HARDY COUNTY,WV"
    1830,  38.965,  79.283,  "GRANT COUNTY,WV"
    1840,  39.033,  80.300,  "UPSHUR COUNTY,WV"
    1850,  38.983,  81.317,  "WIRT COUNTY,WV"
```

```
     1860,   39.008,   82.813,   "PIKE COUNTY,OH"
     1870,   39.200,   83.595,   "HIGHLAND COUNTY,OH"
     1880,   39.069,   84.661,   "BOONE COUNTY,KY"
     1890,   39.199,   85.548,   "DECATUR COUNTY,IN"
     1900,   39.160,   85.815,   "BARTHOLOMEW COUNTY,IN"
     1910,   39.170,   86.539,   "MONROE COUNTY,IN"
     1920,   39.173,   86.721,   "OWEN COUNTY,IN"
     1930,   39.064,   87.135,   "GREENE COUNTY,IN"
     1940,   38.948,   87.376,   "SULLIVAN COUNTY,IN"
     1950,   38.804,   88.369,   "CLAY COUNTY,IL"
     1960,   38.600,   89.210,   "CLINTON COUNTY,IL"
     1970,   38.463,   89.706,   "ST CLAIR COUNTY,IL"
     1980,   38.137,   90.574,   "JEFFERSON COUNTY,MO"
     1990,   37.872,   91.215,   "CRAWFORD COUNTY,MO"
     2000,   37.697,   91.810,   "PHELPS COUNTY,MO"
     ;
run;

* combine the Annotate data set with selected state boundaries from
* the STATES map data set;

data both; ❸
   set
   maps.states (where=(fipstate(state) in ("IA" "IL" "IN" "OH" "PA" "MO"
   "KY" "WV" "VA" "TN" "NC" "MD" "DE" "DC" "AR" "NJ" "NY")
   and density le 3))
   popctr;
run;

* project the combined data set;
proc gproject data=both out=bothproj;
   id state;
run;

* separate the projected Annotate data set from the projected map data set;

data pmap pop;
   set bothproj;
   if when eq 'a' then output pop;
   else                 output pmap;
run;

goptions device=javameta ❹
         gunit=pct
         ftext='HelveticaBold'
         htext=5
         htitle=6;

filename _webout "c:\popcenter.htm";

* write records to an HTML file
* output from the GMAP procedure will be added to the end of the HTML file;❺
```

```
data _null_;
   file _webout;
   input;
   put _infile_;
   datalines;
   <html>
   <head>
   <title>JAVA METAGRAPHICS</title>
   </head>
   <body>
   <applet archive="http://webservername/graph/metafile.zip"
           code="MetaViewApplet.class"
           width="800" height="600" align="TOP">
   <param name="BackgroundColor"    value="0xffffff">
   <param name="ZoomControlEnabled" value="false">
   <param name="Metacodes"          value="
   ;
run;

* a gray-scale fill will be used to fill one state per map;
pattern v=ms c=grayca;

* a macro will be used to create 22 maps - one for each
* year of data in the POPCTR Annotate data set;
%macro manymaps; ❻

* use a macro DO loop to repeat the GMAP procedure 22 times;
%do i=1 %to 22;

* create an Annotate data set with the number of observations controlled
* by the index variable (&i) of the macro DO loop
* when the last observation is reached, create macro variables containing
* values of the variable year, location, and state number;

data anno; ❼
   length text $50;
   set pop (obs=&i) end=last;
   if last then do;
       size = '4';
       text = 'V';
       call symput('year',year);
       call symput('cost',location);
       call symput('fips',put(fips,z3.));
   end;
run;

* use the macro variables &YEAR and &COST in the map title;
title1 "CENTER OF US POPULATION:   &YEAR";
title2 "&cost";

* use the same data set as both the map and response data set
* select one state for the response data set - it will be gray-filled
* the remaining states will only be outlined;
```

```
proc gmap ❽
map=pmap
data=pmap (where=(state=&fips))
all;
    id state;
    choro state / discrete nolegend
                  coutline=black
                  cempty=black
                  annotate=anno;
    run;
quit;

%end;
%mend;

* use the macro to create the maps
* all output from PROC GMAP is written to one file;

%manymaps; ❾

* write more HTML code to complete the file; ❿
data _null_;
    file _webout mod;
    input;
    put _infile_;
    datalines;
    ">
    </applet>
    </body>
    </html>
    ;
run;

filename _webout;
```

A data set is created that contains the locations of the center of the United States population in 10-year increments from 1790 to 2000.❶ In addition to details about the locations (year, longitude and latitude, county, and state), the data set contains a number of other variables (such as FUNCTION and POSITION) that allow it to be used as an Annotate data set.❷ The intent of this data set is to provide the information needed to place three items on each of a series of maps: the year, county, and state as part of the map titles; and a character from the MARKER font at the location of the population center. An Annotate data set can be used to add markers at locations on a map. The longitude and latitude are converted to radians so they may be used to add information to the STATES map data set supplied by SAS. The state number is added to the data set by scanning the location for the two-letter state abbreviation and using the STFIPS function to convert it to a state FIPS code. The annotation information is combined with an unprojected map data set, projected, then split apart from the map.❸

The JAVAMETA device driver is selected, and a FILENAME statement is used to create a fileref (_WEBOUT) for an external HTML file (POPCENTER.HTM) in the local environment (in the directory 'C:\').❹ The JAVAMETA device driver recognizes the fileref _WEBOUT and appends all output from SAS/GRAPH procedures to an external file assigned to _WEBOUT. A DATA step is used to write records to the HTML file.❺ The HTML file specifies the location on the Web server of the applet (METAFILE.ZIP) needed to process the metacodes created by the JAVAMETA device driver and PROC GMAP.

Since 22 maps are to be created using very similar SAS code from map to map, a macro (MANYMAPS) containing a DO loop is written to repeat the use of PROC GMAP.❻ A new Annotate data set (ANNO) is created from observations in the previously created Annotate data set POP during every iteration of the loop.❹ The new data set will contain one observation during the first iteration, two during the second, and twenty-two during the last. The last observation in the new data set contains the information about the population center for the year being displayed: year; county and state name; and state number. These data are placed in macro variables and used in subsequent TITLE statements and in the GMAP procedure. The symbol used to show the population center for the last observation in the new Annotate data set is changed to a star (character "V" in the MARKER font) from the triangle (character "C" in the MARKER font) used to mark previous locations.

PROC GMAP creates the maps.❽ The map data set (PMAP) is used as both the map and response data sets. The state FIPS code for the last state in the Annotate data set is used to select observations from the response data set. This results in only one state being filled with gray while all others are only outlined. The macro is used to create the maps.❾ After the loop is complete and all 22 sets of metacodes are written to the external file POPCENTER.HTM, more statements are added to the HTML file.❿ Notice that the FILE statement uses the MOD option to add to rather than overwrite the file. The fileref _WEBOUT is deassigned at the completion of the job.

In Example 5.5, multiple maps were available in separate files, four files of metacodes produced with the JAVAMETA device driver. A drop-down menu enables you to select a map. When all metacodes for multiple maps are written to one file, two new controls are made available. At the lower left of Figure 5.6 is a control for cycling through the series of maps. At the lower right is a slide-show control. Clicking on the ">" starts a slide show with a user-selected delay between map changes. The twenty-second map is shown in Figure 5.6.

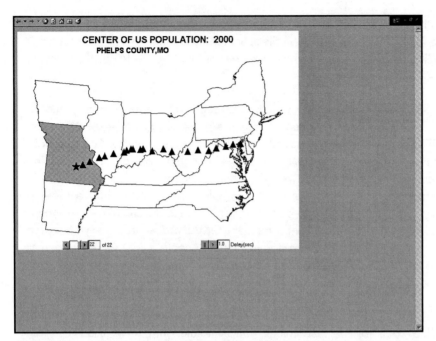

Figure 5.6 *Map with slide-show control (lower right) for animation (JAVAMETA device driver)*

The GIFANIM device driver produces an animated map, but without the on-screen controls produced with the JAVAMETA device driver. However, the animated GIF file is stand-alone and does not require an applet for display.

Example 5.7 Map animation—GIFANIM device driver

```
* create an Annotate data set - used to place a symbol at the location of
* the US population center in each of the years in the DATALINES file;

data popctr; ❶
   retain function 'label' xsys ysys '2' hsys '3' position '5'
          size 3.5 color 'black' style 'marker' text 'C' when 'a';

   infile datalines dsd;
   input year : $4. y x location : $40.;

   fips = stfips(scan(location,-1));
   y    = y*constant('pi')/180;
   x    = x*constant('pi')/180;

   datalines;
   1790,  39.275,  76.187,  "KENT COUNTY,MD"
   1800,  39.268,  76.943,  "HOWARD COUNTY,MD"
   1810,  39.192,  77.620,  "LOUDON COUNTY,VA"
   1820,  39.095,  78.550,  "HARDY COUNTY,WV"
```

```
   1830,   38.965,   79.283,   "GRANT COUNTY,WV"
   1840,   39.033,   80.300,   "UPSHUR COUNTY,WV"
   1850,   38.983,   81.317,   "WIRT COUNTY,WV"
   1860,   39.008,   82.813,   "PIKE COUNTY,OH"
   1870,   39.200,   83.595,   "HIGHLAND COUNTY,OH"
   1880,   39.069,   84.661,   "BOONE COUNTY,KY"
   1890,   39.199,   85.548,   "DECATUR COUNTY,IN"
   1900,   39.160,   85.815,   "BARTHOLOMEW COUNTY,IN"
   1910,   39.170,   86.539,   "MONROE COUNTY,IN"
   1920,   39.173,   86.721,   "OWEN COUNTY,IN"
   1930,   39.064,   87.135,   "GREENE COUNTY,IN"
   1940,   38.948,   87.376,   "SULLIVAN COUNTY,IN"
   1950,   38.804,   88.369,   "CLAY COUNTY,IL"
   1960,   38.600,   89.210,   "CLINTON COUNTY,IL"
   1970,   38.463,   89.706,   "ST CLAIR COUNTY,IL"
   1980,   38.137,   90.574,   "JEFFERSON COUNTY,MO"
   1990,   37.872,   91.215,   "CRAWFORD COUNTY,MO"
   2000,   37.697,   91.810,   "PHELPS COUNTY,MO"
   ;
run;

* combine the Annotate data set with selected state boundaries from
* the STATES map data set;

data both;
   set
   maps.states (where=(fipstate(state) in ("IA" "IL" "IN" "OH" "PA" "MO"
   "KY" "WV" "VA" "TN" "NC" "MD" "DE" "DC" "AR" "NJ" "NY")
   and density le 3))
   popctr;
run;

* project the combined data set;

proc gproject data=both out=bothproj;
id state;
run;

* separate the projected Annotate data set from the projected map data set;

data pmap pop;
   set bothproj;
   if when eq 'a' then output pop;
   else                 output pmap;
run;

goptions device=gifanim ❷
         gsfname=animout
         gsfmode=replace
         gunit=pct
         ftext='Arial/bo'
         ctext=black
         htext=5
         htitle=6
         iteration=0
         delay=200;
```

```
filename animout 'c:\popctr.gif'; ❸

pattern v=ms c=grayca;

%macro manymaps; ❹
%do i=1 %to 22;

%if &i eq  2 %then goptions gsfmode=append;; ❺
%if &i eq 22 %then goptions gepilog='3B'x;; ❻

data anno; ❼
length text $40;
set pop (obs=&i) end=last;
if last then do;
    size = 4;
    text ='V';
    call symput('year' ,year);
    call symput('cost' ,location);
    call symput('fips' ,put(fips,z3.));
end;
run;

title1 "CENTER OF US POPULATION:  &YEAR";
title2 "&cost";

proc gmap
map=pmap
data=pmap (where=(state=&fips))
all;
id state;
choro state / discrete
              nolegend
              coutline=black
              cempty=black
              annotate=anno;
run;
quit;
%end;
%mend;

%manymaps; ❽
```

The same data is used as in Example 5.6, as is the same SAS code up to the point of the GOPTIONS statement.❶ The animated GIF device driver (GIFANIM) is selected, and two options specific to that device driver are used: ITERATION=0 requests that the animation play continuously; DELAY=200 requests that there be a two-second delay between displays of maps (delay units are .01 seconds).❷ The animated GIF file will be created as POPCTR.GIF.❸

A macro is written that runs PROC GMAP 22 times, once for each year in the data set POPCTR.❹ The GSFMODE set prior to execution of the macro is REPLACE. As soon as one map is created, GSFMODE is changed to APPEND.❺ This ensures that a new file will be created each time the macro program is run (replacing any old file named POPCTR.GIF) and that all maps are appended to the new file. Once the last map is written to the GIF file, a hex character "3B" is added to the end of the GIF file using the GEPILOG option.❻ This character is needed as an end-of-file mark in the animated GIF file to make it display properly. The Annotate data set used with the GMAP procedure varies in size depending on the year, and macro variables are used in map titles and to select the state that is filled with gray. The macro is used to create the animated GIF file.

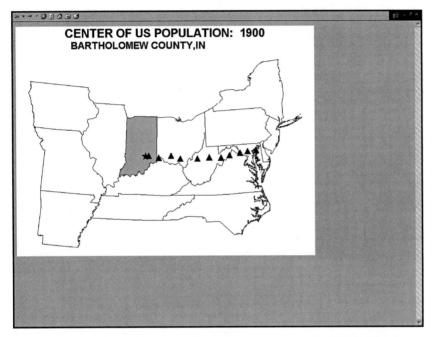

Figure 5.7 *Animated map with no on-screen controls (GIFANIM device driver)*

Figure 5.7 shows the animation at the point of displaying the twelfth map in the sequence. This example makes use of many of the techniques covered in previous examples. The ability to repeat SAS code enclosed within a macro DO loop and to create 22 maps with a minimal amount of effort is another indication of how the use of SAS programming statements enhances the capabilities of displaying information in maps.

Appendix

A1   Data Used in Examples

All the data used in the examples was obtained from the US Census Bureau Web site, http://www.census.gov.

A1.1   United States Population by State

The following SAS code will create the SAS data set US2000ST that is used in a number of the examples. As explained in the text, values of the variable STATE are FIPS codes. STATE is a numeric variable, as is the variable STATE in various SAS/GRAPH map data sets.

```
data us2000st;
   informat region $9. pop2000 pop1990 comma.;
   input state region pop2000 pop1990 @@;
   label
   state   = 'State FIPS Code'
   pop2000 = 'Year 2000 Census Population'
   pop1990 = 'Year 1990 Census Population'
   region  = 'Census Region'
   ;
datalines;
01 SOUTH      4,447,100   4,040,587    02 WEST         626,932     550,043
04 WEST       5,130,632   3,665,228    05 SOUTH      2,673,400   2,350,725
06 WEST      33,871,648  29,760,021    08 WEST       4,301,261   3,294,394
09 NORTHEAST  3,405,565   3,287,116    10 SOUTH        783,600     666,168
11 SOUTH        572,059     606,900    12 SOUTH     15,982,378  12,937,926
13 SOUTH      8,186,453   6,478,216    15 WEST       1,211,537   1,108,229
16 WEST       1,293,953   1,006,749    17 MIDWEST   12,419,293  11,430,602
18 MIDWEST    6,080,485   5,544,159    19 MIDWEST    2,926,324   2,776,755
20 MIDWEST    2,688,418   2,477,574    21 SOUTH      4,041,769   3,685,296
22 SOUTH      4,468,976   4,219,973    23 NORTHEAST  1,274,923   1,227,928
24 SOUTH      5,296,486   4,781,468    25 NORTHEAST  6,349,097   6,016,425
26 MIDWEST    9,938,444   9,295,297    27 MIDWEST    4,919,479   4,375,099
28 SOUTH      2,844,658   2,573,216    29 MIDWEST    5,595,211   5,117,073
30 WEST         902,195     799,065    31 MIDWEST    1,711,263   1,578,385
32 WEST       1,998,257   1,201,833    33 NORTHEAST  1,235,786   1,109,252
34 NORTHEAST  8,414,350   7,730,188    35 WEST       1,819,046   1,515,069
36 NORTHEAST 18,976,457  17,990,455    37 SOUTH      8,049,313   6,628,637
38 MIDWEST      642,200     638,800    39 MIDWEST   11,353,140  10,847,115
40 SOUTH      3,450,654   3,145,585    41 WEST       3,421,399   2,842,321
42 NORTHEAST 12,281,054  11,881,643    44 NORTHEAST  1,048,319   1,003,464
45 SOUTH      4,012,012   3,486,703    46 MIDWEST      754,844     696,004
47 SOUTH      5,689,283   4,877,185    48 SOUTH     20,851,820  16,986,510
49 WEST       2,233,169   1,722,850    50 NORTHEAST    608,827     562,758
51 SOUTH      7,078,515   6,187,358    53 WEST       5,894,121   4,866,692
54 SOUTH      1,808,344   1,793,477    55 MIDWEST    5,363,675   4,891,769
56 WEST         493,782     453,588
;
run;
```

A1.2   United States Population by State and County

The data set US2000CO was created using a US Census Bureau data file. The data set contains 3000+ observations and the following variables:

VARIABLE	TYPE	LABEL
cname	Char	County Name
county	Num	County FIPS Code
pop1990	Num	Census Population in 1990
pop2000	Num	Census Population in 2000
state	Num	State FIPS Code

A1.3   New York Population by County

```
data nys2000co;
informat pop2000 comma.;
input county pop2000 @@;
label
county   = 'County FIPS Code'
pop2000 = 'Year 2000 Census Population'
;
datalines;
001    294,565    003     49,927    005  1,332,650    007      200,536
009     83,955    011     81,963    013    139,750    015       91,070
017     51,401    019     79,894    021     63,094    023       48,599
025     48,055    027    280,150    029    950,265    031       38,851
033     51,134    035     55,073    037     60,370    039       48,195
041      5,379    043     64,427    045    111,738    047    2,465,326
049     26,944    051     64,328    053     69,441    055      735,343
057     49,708    059  1,334,544    061  1,537,195    063      219,846
065    235,469    067    458,336    069    100,224    071      341,367
073     44,171    075    122,377    077     61,676    079       95,745
081  2,229,379    083    152,538    085    443,728    087      286,753
089    111,931    091    200,635    093    146,555    095       31,582
097     19,224    099     33,342    101     98,726    103    1,419,369
105     73,966    107     51,784    109     96,501    111      177,749
113     63,303    115     61,042    117     93,765    119      923,459
121     43,424    123     24,621
;
run;
```

A1.4   *Texas Population by County*

```
data tx2000co;
   informat pop2000 comma.;
   input county pop2000 @@;
   label
   county  = 'County FIPS Code'
   pop2000 = 'Year 2000 Census Population'
   ;
datalines;
001      55,109   003      13,004   005      80,130   007      22,497
009       8,854   011       2,148   013      38,628   015      23,590
017       6,594   019      17,645   021      57,733   023       4,093
025      32,359   027     237,974   029   1,392,931   031       8,418
033         729   035      17,204   037      89,306   039     241,767
041     152,415   043       8,866   045       1,790   047       7,976
049      37,674   051      16,470   053      34,147   055      32,194
057      20,647   059      12,905   061     335,227   063      11,549
065       6,516   067      30,438   069       8,285   071      26,031
073      46,659   075       7,688   077      11,006   079       3,730
081       3,864   083       9,235   085     491,675   087       3,206
089      20,390   091      78,021   093      14,026   095       3,966
097      36,363   099      74,978   101       1,904   103       3,996
105       4,099   107       7,072   109       2,975   111       6,222
113   2,218,899   115      14,985   117      18,561   119       5,327
121     432,976   123      20,013   125       2,762   127      10,248
129       3,828   131      13,120   133      18,297   135     121,123
137       2,162   139     111,360   141     679,622   143      33,001
145      18,576   147      31,242   149      21,804   151       4,344
153       7,771   155       1,622   157     354,452   159       9,458
161      17,867   163      16,252   165      14,467   167     250,158
169       4,872   171      20,814   173       1,406   175       6,928
177      18,628   179      22,744   181     110,595   183     111,379
185      23,552   187      89,023   189      36,602   191       3,782
193       8,229   195       5,369   197       4,724   199      48,073
201   3,400,578   203      62,110   205       5,537   207       6,093
209      97,589   211       3,351   213      73,277   215     569,463
217      32,321   219      22,716   221      41,100   223      31,960
225      23,185   227      33,627   229       3,344   231      76,596
233      23,857   235       1,771   237       8,763   239      14,391
241      35,604   243       2,207   245     252,051   247       5,281
249      39,326   251     126,811   253      20,785   255      15,446
257      71,313   259      23,743   261         414   263         859
265      43,653   267       4,468   269         356   271       3,379
273      31,549   275       4,253   277      48,499   279      14,709
281      17,762   283       5,866   285      19,210   287      15,657
289      15,335   291      70,154   293      22,051   295       3,057
297      12,309   299      17,044   301          67   303     242,628
305       6,550   307       8,205   309     213,517   311         851
313      12,940   315      10,941   317       4,746   319       3,738
321      37,957   323      47,297   325      39,304   327       2,360
329     116,009   331      24,238   333       5,151   335       9,698
337      19,117   339     293,768   341      20,121   343      13,048
345       1,426   347      59,203   349      45,124   351      15,072
353      15,802   355     313,645   357       9,006   359       2,185
361      84,966   363      27,026   365      22,756   367      88,495
```

369	10,016	371	16,809	373	41,133	375	113,546
377	7,304	379	9,139	381	104,312	383	3,326
385	3,047	387	14,314	389	13,137	391	7,828
393	887	395	16,000	397	43,080	399	11,495
401	47,372	403	10,469	405	8,946	407	22,246
409	67,138	411	6,186	413	2,935	415	16,361
417	3,302	419	25,224	421	3,186	423	174,706
425	6,809	427	53,597	429	9,674	431	1,393
433	1,693	435	4,077	437	8,378	439	1,446,219
441	126,555	443	1,081	445	12,761	447	1,850
449	28,118	451	104,010	453	812,280	455	13,779
457	20,871	459	35,291	461	3,404	463	25,926
465	44,856	467	48,140	469	84,088	471	61,758
473	32,663	475	10,909	477	30,373	479	193,117
481	41,188	483	5,284	485	131,664	487	14,676
489	20,082	491	249,967	493	32,408	495	7,173
497	48,793	499	36,752	501	7,322	503	17,943
505	12,182	507	11,600				

```
;
run;
```

A2 SAS Functions for Use with FIPS Codes

Several SAS functions are FIPS code related. The three functions shown in the following program all require a numeric argument. They convert FIPS codes to postal codes or names. Each creates a character variable with a length of 20.

```
data fip_func;
do fips_code = 1 to 95;
   postal = fipstate(fips_code);
   name_u = fipname(fips_code);
   name_m = fipnamel(fips_code);
   if name_u ne : 'INVALID' then output;
end;
label
fips_code = "FIPS CODE"
postal    = 'POSTAL CODE'
name_u    = 'UPPERCASE NAME'
name_m    = 'MIXED CASE NAME'
;
run;

title 'FIPS CODES, POSTAL CODES, NAMES';
proc print data=fip_func noobs label;
run;
```

Some functions convert postal codes either to a numeric FIPS code or to names in upper or mixed case. The functions that return names create character variables with a length of 20. The following program uses the FIPSTATE function to create postal codes, then uses the postal codes with three functions.

```
data st_func;
do fips = 1 to 79;
    postal    = fipstate(fips);
    fips_code = stfips(postal);
    sname_u   = stname(postal);
    sname_m   = stnamel(postal);
    if postal ne '--' then output;
end;
label
fips_code = "FIPS CODE"
postal    = 'TWO-CHARACTER POSTAL CODE'
sname_u   = 'UPPERCASE NAME'
sname_m   = 'MIXED CASE NAME'
;
drop fips;
run;

title 'ST_FUNCTIONS';
proc print data=st_func noobs label;
run;
```

A3   GOPTIONS Statement Used for Examples

The majority of the examples in the book use the following GOPTIONS statement, where the filename is changed as needed:

```
goptions dev=gif gsfname=gout gsfmode=replace
        gunit=pct ftext='Arial' htitle=8 htext=4;
filename gout "choromap.gif";
```

Changes were occasionally made to the FTEXT option, and they are shown using a GOPTIONS statement like the following:

```
goptions ftext='Arial/bo/it';
```

Though not shown in the text, a number of examples also use a LEGEND statement to change the shape of legend boxes when used together with the LEGEND option in PROC GMAP. The following statements define the shape of the legend boxes and then request that the new legend be used when the map is drawn.

```
legend1 shape=bar(3,4);
choro pop2000 / discrete coutline=black legend=legend1;
```

A4 Creating the Gauge Font

PROC GFONT was used to create the gauge font used in Examples 4.5 and 4.6. PROC GFONT stores user-created fonts in a catalog named FONTS in a directory associated with the libref GFONT0. In the following SAS code, the gauge font will be stored in the catalog FONTS in the directory E:\. The first place that SAS looks for fonts is in the GFONT0 library. This libref must be assigned prior to creating and using any user-created fonts.

```
data font;
do i=0 to 100;
   char=input(put(i,hex2.),$2.);

   segment=1;
   lp='p';
   x=0;    y=0;     output;
           y=i;     output;
   x=50;            output;
           y=0;     output;
   x=0;             output;

   segment=2;
   lp='l';
   x=0;    y=0;     output;
           y=100;   output;
   x=50;            output;
           y=0;     output;
   x=0;             output;

   segment=3;
   x=0;    y=50;    output;
   x=-10;           output;

   segment=4;
   x=60;   y=50;    output;
   x=50;            output;
end;
run;

libname gfont0 'e:\';
title 'THE GAUGE FONT';

proc gfont data=font name=gauge filled nokeymap codelen=2 height=3.5;
run;
```

More Information

The SAS code to create the gauge font first appeared in *SAS Observations*, vol. 3, no. 1, 1993, and also appears in SAS Technical Support document TS-398.

A5   Determining the Centroid of Map Areas

In Examples 4.5 and 4.6, symbols were placed at the visual center of states. The information about state centers was found in the data set USCENTER, supplied by SAS. When such information is not available, SAS code can be used to find the visual center of map areas.

```
* MAP - NAME OF MAP DATA SET
* TYPE - VARIABLE THAT IDENTIFIES GEOGRAPHIC AREAS IN MAP (E.G. COUNTY)
* CREATES DATA SET CENTERS;

%macro centroid(map,type);
* CREATE TWO DATA SETS - NUMBER OF POINTS PER AREA AND POINTS;
data
   map(drop=npoints)
   points(keep=x y npoints rename=(x=xlast y=ylast));
   set &map; by &type;
   where x ne .;
   output map;
   npoints+1;
   if last.&type then do;
      output points;
      npoints=0;
   end;
run;

* CALCULATE CENTROIDS;
data
   centers(keep=&type x y rename=(x=xc y=yc));
   retain savptr 1 xold yold 0;
   set points;
   xcg=0; ycg=0;
   aresum=0;
   firstpnt=1;
   endptr=savptr + npoints - 1;
   do ptrm=savptr to endptr;
      set map point=ptrm nobs=nobsm;
      if firstpnt then do;
         xold=x; yold=y;
         savptr=ptrm + npoints;
         firstpnt=0;
      end;
      aretri=((xlast-x)*(yold-ylast)) + ((xold-xlast)*(y-ylast));
      xcg + (aretri*(x+xold));
      ycg + (aretri*(y+yold));
      aresum+aretri;
      xold=x; yold=y;
   end;
   areinv=1.0/aresum;
   x=(((xcg*areinv)+xlast) * (1/3));
   y=(((ycg*areinv)+ylast) * (1/3));
   output;
run;
%mend;
```

More Information

This code first appeared in *SAS Communications*, vol. 13, no. 4, 1998, and is also available in SAS Technical Support document TS-305.

A6   Gray Fills and Color Gradations

Solid, gray-scale fills are used in many of the examples. The appearance of the gray fills will vary slightly from printer to printer. The following SAS code can be used to show all the gray fills on any given output device. Black (gray00) and white (grayff) are not shown.

```
goptions ftext=swissb htext=2 gunit=pct;

* uses the catalog file method to store pattern statements for later
* inclusion in job;
filename tempfile catalog "work.includes.temppatt";

* creates a map (squares) and a data set (temp) to be used in creating
* pattern statements and annotation;

data squares (keep=sq x y)
temp (keep=sq x y);
retain sq 0;
do j = 1 to 16;
do i = 1 to 16;
sq+1;
x=i; y=j; output;
x=i+1; output squares;
y=j+1; output squares;
x=i; output squares;
end;
end;
run;

* eliminate lower-left (white) and upper-right (black) map areas;
data squares;
set squares;
if _n_ gt 4 and _n_ lt 1021 then output;
run;

* create patterns and annotation;
data labels (drop=xy txt);
retain xsys ysys '2' when 'a';
file tempfile;
set temp;
sq = sq - 1;
if 1<=sq<=254;
if x gt 5 then color = 'grayfe';
else color = 'gray01';
```

```
xy = put(16-x,hex1.) || put(16-y,hex1.);
txt = "pattern" || left(trim(put(sq,3.))) || " v=s c=gray" || xy || ";";
put txt;
text=put(xy,2.);
x=x+.5;
y=y+.5;
run;

* include the pattern statements;
%include tempfile;

* create a map with 254 gray-filled areas;
title h=4 "GRAY SCALE FILLS";

proc gmap map=squares data=squares;
id sq;
choro sq/discrete nolegend coutline=gray01 annotate=labels;
run;
quit;
```

GRAY SCALE FILLS

F0	E0	D0	C0	B0	A0	90	80	70	60	50	40	30	20	10	
F1	E1	D1	C1	B1	A1	91	81	71	61	51	41	31	21	11	01
F2	E2	D2	C2	B2	A2	92	82	72	62	52	42	32	22	12	02
F3	E3	D3	C3	B3	A3	93	83	73	63	53	43	33	23	13	03
F4	E4	D4	C4	B4	A4	94	84	74	64	54	44	34	24	14	04
F5	E5	D5	C5	B5	A5	95	85	75	65	55	45	35	25	15	05
F6	E6	D6	C6	B6	A6	96	86	76	66	56	46	36	26	16	06
F7	E7	D7	C7	B7	A7	97	87	77	67	57	47	37	27	17	07
F8	E8	D8	C8	B8	A8	98	88	78	68	58	48	38	28	18	08
F9	E9	D9	C9	B9	A9	99	89	79	69	59	49	39	29	19	09
FA	EA	DA	CA	BA	AA	9A	8A	7A	6A	5A	4A	3A	2A	1A	0A
FB	EB	DB	CB	BB	AB	9B	8B	7B	6B	5B	4B	3B	2B	1B	0B
FC	EC	DC	CC	BC	AC	9C	8C	7C	6C	5C	4C	3C	2C	1C	0C
FD	ED	DD	CD	BD	AD	9D	8D	7D	6D	5D	4D	3D	2D	1D	0D
FE	EE	DE	CE	BE	AE	9E	8E	7E	6E	5E	4E	3E	2E	1E	0E
	EF	DF	CF	BF	AF	9F	8F	7F	6F	5F	4F	3F	2F	1F	0F

Just as the appearance of gray-scale fills varies across output devices, so does the appearance of various colors. There are occasions when map areas are filled with a continuous color gradation—using a single color, starting with a light version, and gradually darkening. The following SAS code uses the RGB color-naming scheme and can be used to illustrate how a given color will appear over 100 different gradations, darkening from left to right. The example starts with light gray, but any color can be used as the starting point by changing the values of the macro variables R, G, and B. For example, light red to dark red could start at R=255, G=200, B=200. This code is derived from a SAS/GRAPH animation example on the SAS Web site and is useful when many color levels are being used to fill map areas, as in Example 2.6, which uses 100 gray-scale patterns.

```
goptions ftext='Arial' gunit=pct;

* set staring values for RED, GREEN, BLUE;
%let r=220;
%let g=220;
%let b=220;

data color100;
retain xsys ysys '3' style 's' xinc 1;
r = &r; rinc = -r/100;
g = &g; ginc = -g/100;
b = &b; binc = -b/100;
x = 0;
do i = .5 to 99.5;
color = 'cx' || put( r, hex2. ) || put( g, hex2. ) || put( b, hex2. );
function = 'MOVE'; y = 10; output;
function = 'BAR' ; x + xinc; y = 90; output;
r + rinc;
g + ginc;
b + binc;
end;
run;

title h=4 "STARTING VALUE: R=&r G=&g B=&b";
proc gslide annotate=color100;
run;
quit;
```

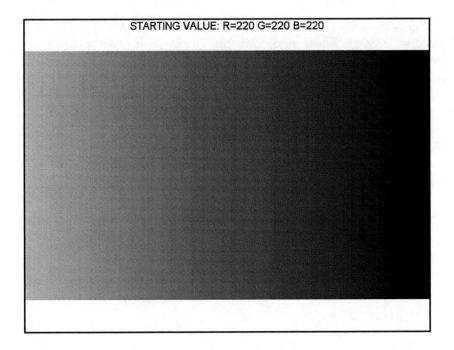

STARTING VALUE: R=220 G=220 B=220

A7   Data Sets Supplied by SAS

Many map data sets are supplied with SAS/GRAPH software. In addition to the map data sets, there are data sets that supply other information. One of these is METAMAPS. This data set contains information about data sets supplied by SAS. The variable list of METAMAPS follows.

VARIABLE	TYPE	LABEL
CONTNENT	Num	Numeric rep for Continent
COUNTRY	Char	Name of Country
EXIST	Num	Installed on Local Machine: 1 or 0
F_GEOCOL	Char	Corresponding GEOREF variable
F_TABLE	Char	Corresponding Feature Table
GISIMPRT	Char	Imports into GIS
LABEL1	Char	Description of Var1 in Dataset
LABEL2	Char	Description of Var2 in Dataset
LABEL3	Char	Description of Var3 in Dataset
LABEL4	Char	Description of Var4 in Dataset

LABEL5	Char	Description of Var5 in Dataset
LABEL6	Char	Description of Var6 in Dataset
LABEL7	Char	Description of Var7 in Dataset
LABEL8	Char	Description of Var8 in Dataset
LABEL9	Char	Description of Var9 in Dataset
LABEL10	Char	Description of Var10 in Dataset
LABEL11	Char	Description of Var11 in Dataset
LABEL12	Char	Description of Var12 in Dataset
LABEL13	Char	Description of Var13 in Dataset
MEMCODE	Char	Dataset Type: G geometry F feature
MEMNAME	Char	Library Member Name
MEMTYPE	Char	Library Member Type
NOBS	Num	Library Member Type
TYPE	Char	Type of Map Dataset: GIS or GRAPH
VAR1	Char	Name of Variable in Dataset
VAR2	Char	Name of Variable in Dataset
VAR3	Char	Name of Variable in Dataset
VAR4	Char	Name of Variable in Dataset
VAR5	Char	Name of Variable in Dataset
VAR6	Char	Name of Variable in Dataset
VAR7	Char	Name of Variable in Dataset
VAR8	Char	Name of Variable in Dataset
VAR9	Char	Name of Variable in Dataset
VAR10	Char	Name of Variable in Dataset
VAR11	Char	Name of Variable in Dataset
VAR12	Char	Name of Variable in Dataset
VAR13	Char	Name of Variable in Dataset

Not all the maps listed in METAMAPS are map data sets. Data sets used with SAS.GIS are also listed. However, map data sets supplied by SAS all contain a variable named SEGMENT. The following can be used to find the names of all the map data sets:

```
data mapdatasets;
set maps.metamaps;
array var(13);
map = 0;
do j=1 to 13;
    if var(j) eq 'SEGMENT' then map = 1;
    if map eq 1 then leave;
end;

if map eq 1 then output;
run;
```

The names of the variables within the map data sets can then be printed:

```
*** print the first 10 names;
proc print data=mapdatasets (obs=10) noobs;
var memname var1-var7;
run;
```

MEMNAME	VAR1	VAR2	VAR3	VAR4	VAR5	VAR6	VAR7
AFGHANIS	ID	LAT	LONG	SEGMENT	X	Y	
AFRICA	CONT	ID	LAT	LONG	SEGMENT	X	Y
ALGERIA	ID	LAT	LONG	SEGMENT	X	Y	
ANDORRA	ID	LAT	LONG	SEGMENT	X	Y	
ARGENTIN	ID	LAT	LONG	SEGMENT	X	Y	
ARMENIA	ID	LAKE	LAT	LONG	SEGMENT	X	Y
ASIA	CONT	ID	LAT	LONG	SEGMENT	X	Y
AUSTRAL	ID	LAKE	LAT	LONG	SEGMENT	X	Y
AUSTRIA	ID	LAKE	LAT	LONG	SEGMENT	X	Y
AZERBAIJ	ID	LAKE	LAT	LONG	SEGMENT	X	Y

Each map data set is paired with another data set that contains information about the variable that names map areas in the map data set. The paired data sets have the same name as the map data set, with a 2 added as a suffix. For example, the map data set AUSTRIA is accompanied by AUSTRIA2. If the map data set name is eight characters long, only the first seven characters are used for the paired data set, again followed by a 2. The exceptions to these naming conventions occur with the Canada data sets and the WORLD data set.

The following output shows the names of the nine map areas in the map data set Austria.

```
proc print data=maps.austria2;
run;

    _MAP_GEOMETRY_        COUNTRY    ID     IDNAME
id 1 of maps.austria       165       1     BURGENLAND
id 2 of maps.austria       165       2     CARINTHIA
id 3 of maps.austria       165       3     LOWER AUSTRIA
id 4 of maps.austria       165       4     SALZBURG
id 5 of maps.austria       165       5     STYRIA
id 6 of maps.austria       165       6     TIROL
id 7 of maps.austria       165       7     UPPER AUSTRIA
id 8 of maps.austria       165       8     VIENNA CITY
id 9 of maps.austria       165       9     VORARLBERG
```

There are two special data sets of use when using annotation to add information to maps of the United States. The first is the USCENTER data set (used in Examples 4.1 and 4.2), which contains the location of the visual center of each state and the District of Columbia. For nine small map areas along the Atlantic coast, there is an extra set of X-Y coordinates that allow a label to be placed to the right of map area (in the ocean). Annotation can then be used to draw a line from the ocean coordinate to the state center.

```
proc contents data=maps.uscenter;
run;
```

VARIABLE	TYPE	LABEL
LAT	Num	Unprojected Latitude in Degrees
LONG	Num	Unprojected Longitude in Degrees
OCEAN	Char	Y or N
STATE	Num	State FIPS Code
X	Num	X Coordinate
Y	Num	Y Coordinate

The second special data set is the USCITY data set (used in Example 4.4), which contains the location of a number of cities and other places. The variable FEATYPE within this data set describes the type of place for which information is provided.

```
proc freq data=maps.uscity;
table featype / nopercent nocum;
run;
```

Type of Place: CDP (Census Designated Place)

FEATYPE	FREQUENCY
CDP	4074
BOROUGH	1169
CITY	9736
TOWN	4780
VILLAGE	3690

Index

Call your local SAS office to order these books
from Books by Users Press

www.sas.com/pubs

Reporting from the Field: SAS® Software Experts Present Real-World Report-Writing Applications . . . . .Order No. A55135

SAS®Applications Programming: A Gentle Introduction
by **Frank C. Dilorio** . . . . .Order No. A56193

SAS® Foundations: From Installation to Operation
by **Rick Aster** . . . . .Order No. A55093

SAS® for Linear Models, Fourth Edition
by **Ramon C. Littell, Walter W. Stroup.**
and **Rudolf Freund** . . . . .Order No. A56655

SAS® Macro Programming Made Easy
by **Michele M. Burlew** . . . . .Order No. A56516

SAS® Programming by Example
by **Ron Cody**
and **Ray Pass** . . . . .Order No. A55126

SAS® Programming for Researchers and Social Scientists, Second Edition
by **Paul E. Spector** . . . . .Order No. A58784

SAS® Software Roadmaps: Your Guide to Discovering the SAS® System
by **Laurie Burch**
and **SherriJoyce King** . . . . .Order No. A56195

SAS® Software Solutions: Basic Data Processing
by **Thomas Miron** . . . . .Order No. A56196

SAS® System for Elementary Statistical Analysis, Second Edition
by **Sandra D. Schlotzhauer**
and **Dr. Ramon C. Littell** . . . . .Order No. A55172

SAS® System for Forecasting Time Series, 1986 Edition
by **John C. Brocklebank**
and **David A. Dickey** . . . . .Order No. A5612

SAS® System for Mixed Models
by **Ramon C. Littell, George A. Milliken, Walter W. Stroup,** and **Russell D. Wolfinger** . .Order No. A55235

SAS® System for Regression, Second Edition
by **Rudolf J. Freund**
and **Ramon C. Littell** . . . . .Order No. A56141

SAS® System for Statistical Graphics, First Edition
by **Michael Friendly** . . . . .Order No. A56143

The SAS® Workbook and Solutions Set
(books in this set also sold separately)
by **Ron Cody** . . . . .Order No. A55594

Selecting Statistical Techniques for Social Science Data: A Guide for SAS® Users
by **Frank M. Andrews, Laura Klem, Patrick M. O'Malley, Willard L. Rodgers, Kathleen B. Welch,** and **Terrence N. Davidson** . . . . .Order No. A55854

Solutions for Your GUI Applications Development Using SAS/AF® FRAME Technology
by **Don Stanley** . . . . .Order No. A55811

Statistical Quality Control Using the SAS® System
by **Dennis W. King, Ph.D.** . . . . .Order No. A55232

A Step-by-Step Approach to Using the SAS® System for Factor Analysis and Structural Equation Modeling
by **Larry Hatcher** . . . . .Order No. A55129

A Step-by-Step Approach to Using the SAS® System for Univariate and Multivariate Statistics
by **Larry Hatcher**
and **Edward Stepanski** . . . . .Order No. A55072

Strategic Data Warehousing Principles Using SAS® Software
by **Peter R. Welbrock** . . . . .Order No. A56278

Survival Analysis Using the SAS® System: A Practical Guide
by **Paul D. Allison** . . . . .Order No. A55233

Table-Driven Strategies for Rapid SAS® Applications Development
by **Tanya Kolosova**
and **Samuel Berestizhevsky** . . . . . . .Order No. A55198

Tuning SAS® Applications in the MVS Environment
by **Michael A. Raithel** . . . . .Order No. A55231

Univariate and Multivariate General Linear Models: Theory and Applications Using SAS® Software
by **Neil H. Timm**
and **Tammy A. Mieczkowski** . . . . . . .Order No. A55809

www.sas.com/pubs

Working with the SAS® System
by **Erik W. Tilanus** . . . . .Order No. A55190

Your Guide to Survey Research Using the
SAS® System
by **Archer Gravely** . . . . .Order No. A55688

JMP® Books

Basic Business Statistics: A Casebook
by **Dean P. Foster, Robert A. Stine,**
and **Richard P. Waterman** . . . . .Order No. A56813

Business Analysis Using Regression: A Casebook
by **Dean P. Foster, Robert A. Stine,**
and **Richard P. Waterman** . . . . .Order No. A56818

JMP® Start Statistics, Second Edition
by **John Sall, Ann Lehman,**
and **Lee Creighton** . . . . .Order No. A58166

www.sas.com/pubs

Welcome * *Bienvenue* * *Willkommen* * *Yohkoso* * *Bienvenido*

SAS Publishing Is Easy to Reach

Visit our Web page located at www.sas.com/pubs

You will find product and service details, including

- **companion Web sites**
- **sample chapters**
- **tables of contents**
- **author biographies**
- **book reviews**

Learn about

- **regional user groups conferences**
- **trade show sites and dates**
- **authoring opportunities**
- **e-books**

Explore all the services that Publications has to offer!

Your Listserv Subscription Automatically Brings the News to You

Do you want to be among the first to learn about the latest books and services available from SAS Publishing? Subscribe to our listserv **newdocnews-l** and, once each month, you will automatically receive a description of the newest books and which environments or operating systems and SAS® release(s) each book addresses.

To subscribe,

1. Send an e-mail message to **listserv@vm.sas.com**

2. Leave the "Subject" line blank

3. Use the following text for your message:

> **subscribe NEWDOCNEWS-L** *your-first-name your-last-name*

For example: subscribe NEWDOCNEWS-L John Doe

You're Invited to Publish with SAS Institute's Books by Users Press

If you enjoy writing about SAS software and how to use it, the Books by Users program at SAS Institute offers a variety of publishing options. We are actively recruiting authors to publish books and sample code.

If you find the idea of writing a book by yourself a little intimidating, consider writing with a co-author. Keep in mind that you will receive complete editorial and publishing support, access to our users, technical advice and assistance, and competitive royalties. Please ask us for an author packet at **sasbbu@sas.com** or call 919-531-7447. See the Books by Users Web page at **www.sas.com/bbu** for complete information.

Book Discount Offered at SAS Public Training Courses!

When you attend one of our SAS Public Training Courses at any of our regional Training Centers in the U.S., you will receive a 20% discount on any book orders placed during the course. Take advantage of this offer at the next course you attend!

SAS Institute Inc.
SAS Campus Drive
Cary, NC 27513-2414
Fax 919-677-4444

E-mail: sasbook@sas.com
Web page: www.sas.com/pubs
To order books, call SAS Publishing Sales at 800-727-3228*
For other SAS Institute business, call 919-677-8000*

* Note: Customers outside the U.S. should contact their local SAS office.

The Power to Know™

SAS Publishing